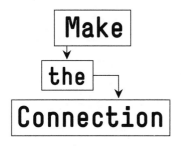

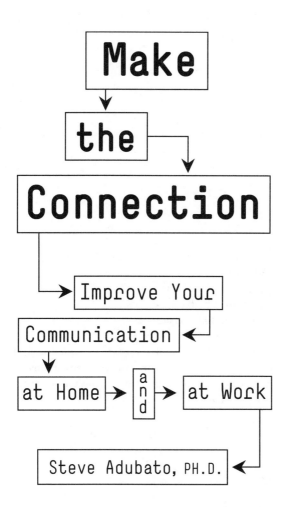

Make
the
Connection

Improve Your

Communication

at Home → and → at Work

Steve Adubato, PH.D.

BARNES
& NOBLE

NEW YORK

This book is dedicated to my three sons:
Stephen, Nicholas, and Christopher,
whom I hope will make the communication connection
at work and at home—better than their father.

CONTENTS

Leadership

Organizational Life

At Work

Motivation

The Customer Is Always Right

Communicating with Strength in Tough Situations

Relationships, Kids, and Communication

Mailbag

ACKNOWLEDGMENTS

This book could not have been written without the support and assistance of many people whom I would like to acknowledge and thank.

Make the Connection is my second book—it's also the second time I have collaborated with Theresa DiGeronimo. While writing *Speak from the Heart,* Theresa was with me every step of the way. Once again, she has helped me to stay focused and on time, and she has forced me to understand that not every column I've written is the masterpiece I wanted to think it was.

Mary Gamba is the head of marketing for our company, Stand & Deliver, but she is really so much more. Not only does she run the company, but every week we work together to meet column deadlines. Mary makes sure those columns are practical and are valuable for our readers. She consistently comes up with important, real-life communication issues. Most important, when I'm "mailing it in" or not giving my best effort, Mary lets me know and guilts me into doing better.

I also want to thank my editors at the *Star-Ledger,* without whom I never would have had the opportunity and challenge of writing about communication and leadership every week for the past five years: Jim Wilse, the *Ledger*'s editor; Kevin Whitmer, the business editor who opened the door for me; and editors Dave Allen and Paul Cox, who have helped me stay fresh and relevant. Thanks, guys. I have obtained releases from individuals quoted at length in the book except when I could not track down the writer, in which case, their names have been masked.

I also want to thank Marlie Wasserman at Rutgers University Press for seeing the value in publishing this book. Some publishers say there are too many books on communication out there, but Marlie realizes that this topic is so complex and important that there are infinite ways of writing about it and helping people "make the connections" that are so important in their lives. And I cannot forget Marlie's copyeditor, Rick Delaney, who worked hard to tighten and polish my work.

My Stand & Deliver clients have been great about allowing me to write about their communication challenges because they know that others will learn from these experiences. For this understanding and generosity I am very appreciative.

Finally, I want to thank my family, including my parents, Fran and Steve Adubato, and also my sisters, Theresa and Michelle, for giving me loads of communication experiences and anecdotes to work with. (Little did they know, it was our "fascinating" childhood growing up in Newark, New Jersey, and the dinner conversations, which for the sake of political correctness I'll call "ethnically spirited," that inspired so many columns on dysfunctional family dynamics and communication.)

I especially want to thank my wife, Jennifer, who has listened to me read early drafts of these columns and so many others whether she wanted to or not. She is a great listener even when she is exhausted from caring for our kids and has only one eye open late at night. It's ironic that I met Jenn eight years ago when as a meeting planner she hired me to speak, pro bono, at an event she had organized. In retrospect, I got paid for that speech in spades. Beyond being smart and candid with her feedback, Jenn has allowed me to write about communication "stuff" that happens at home that so many other couples and families deal with. My wife knows better than most that I don't always practice what I preach as a communication coach and writer. So, to Jenn and my three sons, Stephen, Nick, and Chris, all I can say is that I'm still working to get it right. Thanks for your patience.

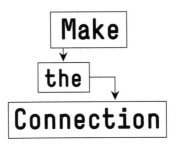

INTRODUCTION

In 1984, as a twenty-six-year-old delegate to the Democratic National Convention in San Francisco, I was mesmerized, along with millions watching on TV, as Mario Cuomo gave the most passionate and memorable convention speech in modern history. I have always been fascinated by people who can make a deep emotional connection through communication. (Years later I would interview Cuomo about that speech for a column that I've included in this book.)

Yet the '84 Cuomo speech is the exception. Most of my experiences have involved situations where people didn't even know there was a "connection" to be made, or when they tried to connect, barriers existed and weren't overcome. Frustration and confusion often followed.

As a state legislator in New Jersey during the mid-80s, I sat through countless mind-numbing speeches on the House floor and during the fourth or fifth hour of legislative committee hearings. Because they gave rambling presentations with no clear message, the speakers were ignored by most senators and representatives. I confess, I often looked for reasons to excuse myself for other "pressing business." I also found that the most effective and most persuasive legislators sometimes listened more and spoke less. Listening is a powerful but too often overlooked communication tool.

As a doctoral student in communication and media studies, I listened to too many "lectures" from smart professors who knew a lot about communication theory but had little ability or desire to connect with students by using probing questions to engage them in a meaningful conversation.

As a media analyst appearing on the Fox News Channel and as a visiting professor at Montclair State University, I examined the 2004 presidential campaign, in which it was rare for any candidate to really connect with voters. Howard Dean's "scream" in Iowa wasn't about passion; it was about a candidate losing control. The biggest reason John Kerry lost was his inability to give people a real sense of who he was and what he believed. His wife, Teresa, never connected with anyone at all. Rather, she turned many people off. And although George Bush won the election, his performances in the debates showed how weak a public communicator he really is.

As a communication coach of leaders in business and the nonprofit sector, I have seen dedicated professionals struggle with preconceived and misinformed notions about public speaking that encouraged them to rely on 110 PowerPoint slides (One of my clients actually tried this) and scripted speeches that invariably put audiences to sleep.

As a broadcaster, I've interviewed too many people who had lots to say and felt the need to try and say it all—without any clear or compelling message. Other times, I've seen confident CEOs and prominent government officials "freeze" with fear when I asked them a question that wasn't expected and therefore without a scripted answer. And I myself experienced a so-called anxiety attack right before interviewing former president George Bush in a live TV event in front of 3,000 people.

It is through these professional and often deeply personal experiences that I've grown as a communication coach and writer. These experiences motivated me to write *Speak from the Heart* in 2002 and now to gather together this collection of columns in *Make the Connection*. In both, the common theme is centered on the need we all have to connect with other people through our daily business and personal interactions.

In this book, I share with you the many questions that I've been asked over and over again by my clients, students, and readers about how to make this much-sought-after connection. The answers explore communication issues and case studies from a variety of professional areas. They reveal my personal life and the dilemmas I've faced over the years as I've struggled to improve my own communication and leadership skills both at work and at home. And they disclose the thoughts, concerns, and insights of my readers who have so kindly and generously written to me since I started writing my communication column for the *Star-Ledger* in February 2000.

The questions that will be answered in this book cover the broad topics of public speaking, workplace interactions, communicating under pressure, the leadership-communication connection, family dynamics, and hi-tech communications. Here's a peek at what you'll find.

Public Speaking

From local PTA meetings to presidential addresses, we all find ourselves in the spotlight sooner or later. Yet, speaking in public is still the most feared form of communication. In this book, you'll find answers to questions such as:

- Why does public speaking cause so much anxiety and fear?
- Why do even professional speakers (myself included) sometimes experience stage fright?
- Why is it that the message sent is rarely the message received?
- How can I keep my audience interested and make sure they don't fall asleep while I'm talking?
- When I do speak in public, what do I do with my hands?
- Why can't I just read off my index cards like I did so well in the third grade?

Workplace Interactions

Unless you work at home without a phone, fax, or computer, you spend an inordinate amount of time communicating with others about work-related issues. Therefore, it's essential to learn how to get your point across without polarizing colleagues, employees, and clients. You need answers to questions such as:

- Why is it so difficult to give constructive, valuable feedback to colleagues without making them feel defensive?
- How can I negotiate a good deal and still be honest and straight?
- How can multitasking get in the way of effective communication?

- What's the best way to give a verbal pat on the back?
- Why do team projects so often fall apart?

Communicating under Pressure

The challenge to be a strong communicator increases when the going gets tough. Donald Trump may revel in saying "You're fired" for the cameras, but the rest of us often squirm and delay when confronting difficult situations. We need answers to questions such as:

- What's the best way to publicly handle a crisis-driven situation in a world dominated by an omnipresent news media, obsessed with playing the "gottcha" game?
- What was so wrong with Martha Stewart's communication strategy?
- Why was the response of the Catholic Church to its sex abuse scandal bound to be a PR disaster?
- What can I learn from Governor James McGreevey's resignation crisis?
- How can I confront a problem employee without being contentious?
- How do I respond to a public insult?

The Leadership-Communication Connection

All great leaders know the power of words to touch the hearts of others. They also know the importance of being a superb listener. Now you will, too.

- Are great communicators born with the gift of communication skills? Or are they trained?
- What was it about retired Lieutenant Colonel Hank Keirsey that pushed him to step up and take responsibility as a military leader even though he wasn't personally responsible for the mistakes that were made by a member of his team?

- What makes people like Bill Clinton, Rudy Giuliani, Mario Cuomo, Jack Welch, and Joe Torre so good at connecting with their audience? What can we learn from them?
- Is Bill Parcells's style of confrontational leadership right for you?
- Why is it so difficult for some leaders to take responsibility for their actions, say "I'm sorry," and mean it?
- Can great leaders also be good friends?

Family Dynamics

Communicating at home with your spouse and children is no less important or any less difficult than communicating in public or at work. There are so many pressing questions we all struggle with as we work each day to share a bit of ourselves, our feelings, beliefs, hopes, and dreams with those we love.

- How can we more effectively communicate with our kids about the horrors of war and terrorism when they see countless graphic images on TV and in other forms of media?
- How can we avoid those stupid arguments with spouses, siblings, and other family members? (I'm still working on that one.)
- How can we use words and breathing to better manage anger?
- Are women really more empathetic than men?
- Is nagging the best form of persuasion we've got?

Hi-Tech Communication

Technology has forever changed the way we communicate. Unfortunately, the benefits of quicker and more visual communication are too often lost when hi-tech bells and whistles get in the way of making a more personal and human connection. We need to know:

- How can I use PowerPoint in my presentation and still engage my audience?

- Why do we hide behind e-mail messages when we have some-thing very difficult to say, even though we know this is so im-personal and so easily misunderstood?
- How can I stay focused on the person I'm talking to when my cell, fax, and e-mail are all calling for my attention?
- Is a simultaneous electronic memo appropriate for important messages?

Mailbag Contributions

Some of my answers to these questions have prompted strong reactions from my readers. In one of my columns, for example, I referred to the movie *A League of Their Own,* in which the team manager (played by Tom Hanks) yelled at his player who had just made an inning-killing mistake, "There's no crying in baseball!" I then wrote that there's also "no crying in business." Lots of professional women wrote me poison pen let-ters expressing the feeling that I was all wet on that one. These letters and others like them are included in this book to share the beliefs of others on this important human need called communication.

Make the Connection is a collection of my most compelling and useful writings on these subjects. They contain the information that I have found most helpful in my communication and leadership coaching over the years. Simply put, the chapters in this book are the best I have to offer.

You can read through them in several ways. Cover-to-cover is fine, but you can also pick and choose the chapters that you think will be most helpful in dealing with the pressing communication challenge facing you today. So read on and enjoy. In the process, I'm confident you'll find something useful about how communication does and does not work. You'll learn more about yourself and how you interact with the people who matter most at work and at home.

Steve Adubato, Ph.D.
January 2005

Communication 101

Chapter 1

MESSAGE SENT DOES NOT EQUAL MESSAGE RECEIVED

What is effective communication? We talk about it all the time, but what does it really mean? I define effective communication as message sent (MS) equals message received (MR). Sounds simple enough, right? Fact is, more times than not message sent does NOT equal message received. Put another way, ineffective communication is a lot more common than effective communication. One of the biggest reasons MS doesn't equal MR is that too often we assume that the people we speak to must have understood us, when the fact is they didn't.

After explaining something, we often ask, "Do you understand?" Of course that person says, "yes." But do people really get the messages we send? You assume they understand, and they think they've got it correct, and you all go on your way with totally different interpretations of what just took place. Later, you find out you were miles apart. But making incorrect assumptions is only one of many reasons for miscommunication. Here are some other reasons:

- Limited attention span of the listener. Think about it. Look at the way we flip from channel to channel when watching television. If what we see doesn't grab our attention in the first few seconds, we "click," on to the next channel. The same thing is true when we are listening to someone. If the topic doesn't grab our attention immediately, we are on to a different channel thinking about where we'd rather be, what we'd rather be doing, or when this guy will stop talking. The best communicators are aware of their audience's limited attention span and get to the point and stay on the point—and stick with it.

- Ambiguous language. What does it mean when someone says, "I'll be there right away," or "This restaurant is not too expensive"? This sort of vague or ambiguous language is a prescription for misunderstanding and confusion. Your best bet is to use more precise, mutually agreed upon language that limits the potential for different interpretations. Consider this as an alternative, "I'll be there in five minutes" or "You can get a great meal for two for less than $60."

- Use of jargon. I used to think that it was just doctors, lawyers, and scientists who used unnecessary jargon or language that only their peers understood. Fact is, car salesmen, accountants, and computer experts are also obsessed with their own jargon. Why do we think the average person would understand words that are unique to a specialized field or profession? Using jargon turns people off and leaves them in the dark. Effective communicators find words, phrases, analogies, and examples to get their message across regardless of their audience's background, education, or training.

- Cultural differences. We live in a very diverse world where not only words but also nonverbal communications are interpreted differently depending upon where people are from and what their culture has taught them. It is impossible to know the verbal and nonverbal nuances of every ethnicity or culture, but it is wrong to be oblivious to our differences and to the fact that our way of communicating may not be universally understood.

- Distracting body language. You can be making the most compelling point or argument while your body language distracts your listener and distorts your intent. If a speaker is rocking back and forth or fidgeting with the change in his or her pocket, it's hard to pay attention to what is being said. If a friend or colleague is saying that he really cares about what you are telling him, but appears to be looking right past you, which message is received? Is it genuine concern or outright apathy? Our body language speaks volumes and must be in sync with what comes out of our mouths.

Chapter 2

CONNECTING MEANS TAKING RISKS

Great communication comes from a combination of practice, persistence, and patience. It also comes from a burning desire to connect with other people in a more meaningful, personal fashion.

Recently, I had the opportunity to speak with one of the more charismatic, and no doubt effective, communicators in the world of business. Charles Hamm is the recently retired president and CEO and currently chairman of a major New York- based bank that does a lot of business in New Jersey. When I interviewed Mr. Hamm for public television, I was struck by his ability to articulate in a clear, concise, and compelling fashion. He used powerful anecdotes and spoke in a conversational fashion. He was so good that I felt compelled to ask him how he got to be that good. "Were you born with it?" "Did it come naturally?" "Were you a big talker as a kid?" Charles Hamm's response shocked me.

"I was dyslexic," he said. "I couldn't read or write. I struggled through school and just barely made it through, albeit the best schools around. I was quiet and remote. And the reason was because I was worried about speaking. Everything was backwards or upside down: D's and B's and Q's and G's. They put my homework on the board and made fun of it. I learned to listen. I was so afraid to communicate that I absorbed everything."

Eventually, Hamm became a top-level executive in advertising and marketing. Yet, despite how much he absorbed he continued to be afraid to speak in public because of his dyslexia and his childhood memories. For more than two decades, Hamm would write out his speeches—but then have problems reading them afterward. It was then that he made the decision that not only changed his career, but literally changed his life. He decided to face his fear head-on.

"At the advice of a speech therapist, I decided to swallow my fear. I threw out the fear, threw out the notes and went up shaking like a leaf and did it. And I've never stopped."

Hamm decided to go with what he knew and, in fact, speak from the heart. Instead of getting confused and overwhelmed by a mass of numbers, statistics, and data, he took a more personal and human approach to the way he spoke in front of others, whether at a meeting, a presentation, or putting together a one-on-one deal. "What I try to do is understand the subject, be passionate about it, understand what the essence of that subject means to someone else and then give it to them. I just expose myself as an emotional commitment to an idea."

I asked Hamm to respond to those in the banking or any other business who are convinced that speaking in a more informal and personal fashion is risky and choose instead to communicate in purely rational, logical, and bottom-line terms. "Rationality and logic do not rule the world. It's an excuse. Emotion rules the world."

Like millions of others who were born with certain challenges and obstacles, Charles Hamm overcame dyslexia and painful shyness to become a giant communicator in the world of industry. But that doesn't happen by osmosis. He made it a priority in his life. He decided to take a risk. Charles Hamm is undoubtedly a communication all-star.

Chapter 3

BODY LANGUAGE SPEAKS VOLUMES

A business executive is undergoing a "mock" media interview. He is preparing for a real media interview he is about to face. The executive's message is clear, and his content is solid. The problem is that as he speaks, his legs are tightly crossed, and he is clutching his left shoe, apparently holding on for dear life. He then proceeds to wring his hands and crack his knuckles. Worst of all, his eyes dart all over the room, looking anyplace other than where they should be. Simply put, his nonverbal communication is a mess.

What he says with his body speaks so loudly, his words become almost nonrelevant. That's the thing with nonverbal communication. Not only is it extremely powerful in how others perceive us, but most of us are oblivious to the messages we are sending. Studies indicate that nearly 90 percent of how we are perceived by others is directly related to body language as opposed to what we actually say.

When I mentioned this problem to the executive, he said, "I was really nervous and wasn't paying attention to anything other than what I said." When he saw himself on videotape, he was shocked. Consider some of the following nonverbal issues that could help your next communication experience:

- Posture. Lots of people are either way too stiff or wind up slouching or hunching their shoulders. The key is to stand or sit straight, but try to be relaxed in the process.
- The handshake. If you currently use what is commonly called the "fish" shake, change it. A weak handshake communicates uninterest. Conversely, you don't need to break knuckles to prove you are a serious leader. A firm handshake will do.
- Hand placement. Instead of wringing your hands, or cracking your knuckles, or, worse yet, locking your hands in one position or place, try another approach. Consider using softer hands. Bring them together lightly touching your two index fingers and gently clasping the rest of your fingers. Then, as you speak, don't be afraid to use your hands to express a point you are making. If you feel strongly about what you are saying, your hands will naturally follow, but they can't follow if you've got them locked up.
- Rocking. Most people rock back and forth without even realizing it. To make sure you don't rock, set your feet on the ground, whether standing or sitting. Square your shoulders and center your torso. If you have to move to get rid of nervous energy, then do it in a more productive and constructive

fashion. Incorporate movement into the presentation by simply standing up or walking around.

- Facial expression. Too many people communicate negative messages through clenched jaws, sneers, or frowns. If you intend to communicate a negative message, then go right ahead and use your face. But, if you think you're fooling anyone about how you really feel, you're not.
- Eye contact. The eyes really are the windows of the soul. We often complain of shifty eyes. We notice when a person "can't look me in the eye." These nonverbal eye contact issues create real problems in our everyday communication. Get into the practice of looking at the person you are interacting with. Steady, focused but relaxed eye contact is the goal.

Chapter 4

MUSHY MESSAGES DON'T CUT IT

Have you ever noticed that some people in the workplace have a tendency to use mushy language? I'm talking about senior-level executives and others who give a presentation and say things like: "I think if we possibly move forward on Project X, we might be able to accomplish our goals in the not so distant future." What's that supposed to mean?

I am amazed at how many otherwise competent professionals communicate using such lame language. I'm not sure where it comes from or what's driving it, but it seems that some people have a tendency to couch their statements in a less than candid or direct fashion. Maybe it's about hedging bets or trying not to put people on the spot. The problem is that when we speak with all of these unnecessary qualifiers, we communicate a variety of misleading messages that we don't intend.

More than four decades ago, President John F. Kennedy made it crystal clear that his goal (in fact our country's goal) was to put a U.S. astronaut on the moon by the end of the decade. It was no accident that this happened. Real leadership requires that those in charge clearly state an organization's goal in an unequivocal fashion. Imagine if JFK had said at the time, "I don't know. . . . It would be nice if we might be able to possibly put one of our guys on the moon maybe sometime soon." If JFK had communicated in this fashion, how committed would the rest of the nation have been? We need to believe that our leaders believe in what they are saying.

Most people who use these mushy words and phrases are often not even aware they are doing it. I've had clients in communication seminars or in executive coaching sessions who are stunned when they see and hear themselves on video saying, "I think," "maybe," or "possibly" over and over again.

Unfortunately, bad communication habits have been engrained into our psyche and presentation styles to the point where they have become second nature. It is the same with presenters who utter "um" and "ah" incessantly without ever knowing they are doing it until it is pointed out to them. If you think these qualifying words and phrases are no big deal, think again. If you only "think" a particular idea is the right way to go, what am I as your audience supposed to think? I need to *know* that you believe in what you are saying in order for there to be any chance I am going to buy in.

If you really aren't sure what you are saying, then make that clear. It's okay not to be sure and to seek input or feedback on a possible decision or action, but that's not what's happening here. Professionals who say they are clear in the direction they want to go are consistently communicating in vague, ambiguous, and ultimately confusing ways.

So what do we do about all this? The first thing is to acknowledge that you are actually doing it. Go ahead, use a camcorder or audiocassette recorder to tape your next presentation and then listen to how you sound. If you are communicating using mushy messages, start practicing making clear, unambiguous, and confident statements. By doing this, you will automatically eliminate words and phrases such as, "I think." And if you do hear yourself using such language, try this approach: "I think . . . no, I *know* that if we move forward in this direction, we will accomplish our goals in the next sixty days."

Great leaders leave little to interpretation.

Chapter 5

LOSE THE JARGON NO ONE UNDERSTANDS

"We are the industry leader in providing a total visibility in the value chain using multi-layered technology that is inter-operable across platforms. . . . Our center-to-edge solution acts as a virtual e-Hub allowing proactive, agile responses throughout your ecosystem. . . . Our best-of-breed collaborative commerce application is robust and highly scalable."

This is an actual combination sales pitch and vendor product press release from an e-commerce trade show. I dare you to tell me what exactly is being said by it. In a powerful editorial in *Supply Chain E-Business,* a popular trade journal, editor Thomas Foster argues that this type of pitch amounts to nothing more than "cyber-babble" that serves to confuse and turn off the intended audience. In dissecting the sales pitch, Foster asks, "What exactly is collaborative commerce (CC)? How is supply-chain process management (SCPM) different from supply-chain performance management (SCPM)?" Finally, Foster asks, why is his industry so uniformly bad at explaining what their applications are supposed to accomplish? All great questions that cry out for answers but too often go ignored by those who practice such *obfuscation.* (Okay, I would never use that word either, but I am just trying to prove a point. FYI, according to *Webster, obfuscation* is defined as "to make obscure and/or confuse.")

It's amazing. In such an intensely competitive environment and with our economy on shaky ground, all professionals need to make a more direct, powerful, and lasting connection with their market audience. They need to do everything possible to make the customer work as little as possible in connection with a business transaction. Our emphasis needs to be on simplification of our language and practical application of our product or service. Why, then, do so many professionals, from the cyber world to government administrators, from car salesmen to financial analysts still employed on Wall Street, engage in this absurd communication approach filled with acronyms, insider jargon, and frustratingly indirect and unclear language?

I have long argued that it is because these communicators are largely clueless as to how they are being received or not received by their audience and lack the skills and tools necessary to communicate more effectively. Further, these folks lack the empathy needed to imagine what it might be like to be on the other end of such a verbal onslaught. I still think I'm right. However, Tom Foster has offered a different explanation when it comes to his particular field: "I honestly think the whole cyber-babble thing is intentional. Many vendors simply do not want their marketing messages to be clear and understandable for marketing purposes. This may sound cynical, but consider the following: A vague product statement will force a prospect to ask for greater detail, which means there is an opportunity for a face-to-face sales pitch."

I don't buy it. Those who believe that they are going to entice or attract prospective clients and customers because of such techno-jargon are dead wrong. To prove my point, reread the opening paragraph of this chapter and ask yourself if one of the first things you would do is get on the phone or e-mail those who put out this convoluted message and ask for a "face to face" meeting so they can decipher and decode it? Or, would you fall over laughing while reading it to your colleagues? Write to me, I'd love to know. Bottom line, the old adage "keep it simple" has never been more accurate than it is today.

Chapter 6

WHEN LESS IS MORE

People often say the problem in an organization is "not enough communication." But it is rarely more information that's needed—it's more effective and relevant information that's missing from our communication today.

The Internet is filled with lots of information, but how much of it is actually pertinent to our lives? Cable TV offers nearly one hundred or more channels—lots of choices, lots of information. But how much of it can we really use? Of the e-mails we get, how many of them are junk? Whether it's the Internet, television, or the reams of memos and e-mails that inundate us, we are constantly trying to manage and make sense of the information and data in our lives.

One of the biggest mistakes people make when giving oral presentations is that they simply have too much data or too many facts. They don't realize that the more information they try to cram into the heads of their audience, the more likely it is that they will lose, confuse, and in fact bore that audience. Remember: less is usually more.

Research shows that the vast amount of information that you communicate in a speech or presentation will be forgotten by most of your audience within five minutes. Further, much of what people are convinced they remember, they remember incorrectly. Just as a columnist must edit his writing to fit the allotted space in a newspaper, the same is true of a presenter. So next time you have to give a presentation, consider cutting it down by at least half. If you plan to speak for twenty minutes, speak only for ten.

Further, our minds hate confusion. General Electric's former CEO Jack Welch best described this issue in an interview in the *Harvard Business Review:* "Insecure business managers create complexity . . . with busy slides filled with everything they've known since childhood."

Welsh has it right. We often present too much information in order to show how smart we are. Well, most people aren't impressed. They just think we're trying to tell them everything we know rather than thinking about the information they might actually care about or find relevant. But doing "data dumps" continues to be the norm in too many organizations.

We are convinced that the more voluminous a presentation or report, the more likely we are to get positive feedback. It's just like in college or high school, when the teacher asks you to write a term paper that is no longer than ten pages, and all the high achievers submit one that is twenty pages. They delude themselves into thinking that twenty pages equal an automatic A. Rarely does it work that way. Particularly when the teacher can't figure out what the point is. I'm convinced we give long speeches and write lengthy term papers because we think doing so implies that we did a lot of work. In truth, that approach is often the product of laziness. The hard work is in editing, cutting down, and prioritizing communication. This comes down to making tough choices and asking ourselves some hard questions about what is really important both to us and our audience.

Finally, as former Apple Computer chairman John Sculley says, simplicity is the "ultimate sophistication." How true. My advice? Start editing right away. Your audience will appreciate it.

Chapter 7

COMMUNICATION: A MATTER OF LIFE AND DEATH

Quality communication skills are crucial to quality health care, and Peter Pronovost, medical director of the Center for Innovations in Quality Patient Care at Johns Hopkins University, says failure to communicate costs lives and money.

Consider the following insights offered by Pronovost, who is one of the country's top experts on reducing medical errors through communication training:

- Nearly 90 percent of every error, not just in health care but in every industry, is about communication.
- Many of these problems stem from a "hierarchical culture" obsessed with who is doing the talking as well as the listening. For example, Dr. Pronovost found that sometimes doctors ignore information from nurses, and pilots ignore direction from copilots, solely because the information is coming from a "subordinate." How many CEOs and other top executives ignore the advice of those who report to them?
- Much of this hierarchical culture problem is subconscious, meaning those who ignore important information from those "beneath" them often don't even realize they are doing it. It's an attitude and philosophy that is engrained in people over many years and countless experiences in organizational bureaucracies.

- Because of this organizational phenomenon, those who are ignored often stop communicating or sharing valuable information because they feel their voice is irrelevant.

To address these serious issues, Dr. Pronovost and his colleagues at Johns Hopkins have developed a three-step communication strategy that he calls an "assertiveness model":

1. When you have a particular concern or want to express an opinion, get someone's attention by using his or her first name. For example, a nurse might say to a doctor, "John, the patient's platelet count is low." Pronovost argues that using a doctor's first name helps break down artificial barriers and the hierarchical culture that often impedes effective communication.
2. State exactly what you believe should be done to remedy the situation and seek agreement. ("I would like to transfuse platelets. Can we agree on that?") Don't assume you have been understood or that you are on the same page with someone else until you've heard a verbal response to that effect. If there is no response, repeat what you've said.
3. Finally, if there is no agreement, bump it up the chain of command and make it clear that your objective is to make sure you communicate clearly and effectively.

While Dr. Pronovost coaches and trains in the field of medicine, this communication "assertiveness model" has value in any professional setting. The goal is to reduce the risk of miscommunication and hold ourselves to a higher standard in the way we engage others in the workplace. Anything less is unacceptable.

Chapter 8

THE Q & A

Too often a simple question in the workplace gets a rambling, complicated, and confusing answer. Here are some tangible tips about how to answer clearly and concisely for improved communication:

- Don't accept the negative premise of a question. Say you get asked something like: "Why is your system of delivering services so complicated and confusing?" Now, assuming you believe in the system in place, turn the negative premise on its head and respond with: "If you are asking me why we have so many checks and balances and safeguards built into the system, the answer is to protect our customers. Let me explain . . ."
- Don't fall in the trap of multipart questions. The best approach is not to try to answer all of the questions that have been posed of you. Option one is to answer the question you are most comfortable with. "You've posed several questions. Let me take the one about why I recommended this particular approach. . . ." Another option is to turn the question around and answer with a follow-up question. "John, as you know you have asked me several questions. Which one is most important to you and why?" The key is not to get bogged down in a long-winded multipart answer.
- Always offer an example in your answer. Even though you've stated your point and may have even provided some details, including facts, figures, and other background information, sometimes a simple, concrete, and relevant example will make an answer resonate and connect with your questioner. For example: "We were meeting with one of our clients last week who was using our XYZ product and he was saying how it has helped them cut their production costs by over 30 percent in the last six months. . . ."
- If you are asked to speculate or hypothesize, use great caution. Too often hypothetical questions are dangerous traps. For one

thing, when the questioner repeats your response, he often won't clarify that you were responding to a hypothetical question. Further, there are too many variables that make speculating or hypothesizing dangerous. When you're asked to answer this type of question, make it clear that you believe that answering hypothetical questions is dangerous and then qualify your answer this way: "Jane, as you know you have asked me a hypothetical question. Now, assuming all things were to stay the same, which is a very big assumption, here is how I see it. . . ." Then, remind Jane that if circumstances change, so would your answer.

- Sometimes, you can be asked a rambling, complicated, and confusing closed-ended question that requires a simple "yes" or "no." If you are, then don't hesitate to respond that way. Never underestimate the eloquence of a simple, concise answer.

Chapter 9

THE POWER OF QUESTIONS

Too often we ignore the value of asking smart, probing, illuminating questions—mostly because we've been trained to focus only on answers. Many of us are obsessed with coming up with the right answers to difficult problems in the workplace. In school, students are taught to come up with the correct answers in order to get a good grade. Clearly, answers are important, but so are questions and they are too often taken for granted. Even if you've taken a course in communications or public speaking, you probably never incorporate questions into your presentations. Yet, lawyers, managers, teachers, doctors, and, yes, journalists, depend heavily on good questioning techniques to do their jobs.

With this in mind, consider some keys to getting more out of the questions you ask both at home and at work:

- Make sure your questions are clear and easy to understand. Sounds simple, right? Then why is it that too often people will ask a question and you have no idea what they want to find out? Before you ask a question, make sure you know why you are asking it.
- Direct your questions to a particular person. Questions asked of particular people are more effective than simply asking a question of an entire group, because you are more likely to get a direct response. Often, when questions are asked of an entire group, people are reluctant to be the first to speak up, and this method also makes it easier for audience members to hide and not participate.
- One at a time. Don't you hate those "three-part questions?" How do you know which part you are supposed to answer first? Did you ever notice that you can't remember what the first part was? Ask one question on one subject to one person and you'll be pleased with the results.
- Follow up on a previous question that has been responded to. Something like, "Mary, how does your answer compare with what Jim said on this subject earlier in the meeting?" Another effective follow-up is a quickie encourager after someone has responded to an initial question, like, "How so?" or "For example. . . ."
- Questions shouldn't be overly confrontational (unless, of course, you have a good reason). "Why is it that you never seem to get it right, Bob?" If you are looking to scare the heck out of Bob or let him know he is about to be fired, you've succeeded. Questions like this can cause real communication problems.

Asking the right questions is very important. In some situations it can even save your life. That's the message from Dorothy Leeds, author of the book *The Seven Powers of Questions* (Perigee, 2000). You might call Leeds the queen of questions. She has spent much of her professional life trying to understand how questions fit into the communication equation. She should know. In 1982 Leeds was diagnosed with breast cancer. After a mammogram, her doctor came in to the room and said simply,

"Dorothy, your tumor is malignant." He was prepared to do a radical mastectomy, but she kept asking, "What are my options? . . . There are always options, aren't there?" Because of her persistent questioning of different doctors, she found one who said a lumpectomy was the way to go. That doctor was right, but none of this would have happened if Dorothy hadn't asked the right questions. Over twenty years later, Dorothy Leeds is still asking the right questions.

What about you? Think about how you can make better use of questions in your everyday communication and actively try to do it.

Chapter 10

THE "FUNNEL" APPROACH

Asking questions is an art form. That's why it's no surprise that the most effective professionals in sales, customer service, or counseling are those who truly understand how to ask questions.

One of the most effective questioning techniques is called the "funnel" approach. Picture what a funnel looks like—wide at the top and narrow at the bottom. The idea is to ask broad, very general questions at the beginning and continue to narrow the focus of your questions with greater specificity. Your goal is to draw out your audience, be it one or one hundred, in an effort to capture their true wants, hopes, and needs.

Your first question opens the door. You want to get the other person talking. Consider some general questions that achieve this goal:

- What do you like most about your work?
- What goals do you and your organization want to accomplish over the next six months?
- How do you see your personal and/or professional life changing over the next several years?

Then listen to what is said and make sure the next questions you ask tap into what you've heard. Start narrowing the funnel. For example, if someone responds to the question about what he likes most about his work by saying, "I enjoy the challenges I face on a daily basis and the opportunity to take risks," a logical follow-up question would be, "That's great, George. Can you tell me of a recent challenge you've had in the last month or so?" That's going from the general to the specific.

Next you get even more specific as you move closer to the bottom of the funnel. You might ask, "What was the reaction of those around you to how you took on the challenge?" Or, "When you took on that risk, what was your greatest fear or concern?" Then finally, at the bottom of the funnel, you might ask, "What's the biggest lesson you've taken away from this?" As you can see, the questions become more and more specific.

As you move down the funnel, resist the urge to jump around to different topics or other lines of questioning that have nothing to do with the area you are attempting to explore. One of the biggest questioning mistakes people make is to ask questions without a game plan. They are all over the map. It is as if they think that magically they are going to unearth some crucial information from a customer with this haphazard technique. Well, it is not going to happen. You can't have several funnels going on at the same time.

The funnel approach of questioning is also extremely helpful in solving problems, identifying opportunities, and resolving conflict. Consider this. If you are in a debate with someone, what do you accomplish by simply arguing the same point over and over again? Usually nothing. So, instead of arguing, ask a question: "Jim, I want to understand this. If we do what you propose, what impact do you think it will have on our customers?" The goal is to get out of argument mode and move to a more productive dialogue with Jim. A probing question is a great way of switching gears. Then, once Jim responds, you can proceed with the funnel approach by asking a more specific question.

Simply put, questions are powerful, so how you ask them should be taken seriously. Try the funnel approach with some sticky issue or challenge at work or at home. If you stay on topic and ask specific questions that gradually narrow in focus, you'll find your communication skills dramatically improve.

Chapter 11

GEORGE BUSH—THE FATHER— LEARNS NEW TRICKS

Former president George Bush was never known to be a powerful public speaker. His communication skills were the butt of many jokes. *Saturday Night Live* had a field day poking fun when Bush would misspeak or fumble over his words. Ronald Reagan or Bill Clinton, George Bush wasn't.

Fast forward. Former President Bush has dramatically improved his communication skills. In 2003, Bush delivered the keynote address at Cingular Wireless's national convention in Las Vegas. After his speech, I moderated a conversation with the president on the topics of leadership and communication. Both in his "formal" remarks and his Q & A responses, Bush was on his game. His style was engaging and relaxed, filled with serious and sensitive anecdotes, personal observations and spontaneous reactions to questions. He was conversational and funny and the audience (some of whom were skeptical before the speech) loved it.

One of the first things Bush did was to tell his audience of "techies" that he had become addicted to a personalized wireless organizer called Blackberry. He talked about all the ways it had improved his communication on a regular basis. Yet, he also poked fun at his technical abilities, saying he still didn't know how to shut off the blinking green light on his TV/VCR. He told a story about how much Barbara Bush, who was also in attendance, was the real leader of the Bush family. The former president said his son George was over at the house recently and the three of them were hanging around talking. George put his feet up on the furniture and his mother immediately chastised him, saying, "George, get your feet off the furniture." The former president turned to his wife and said, "Barbara, you can't talk to him that way, he is the president of the United States," to which Mrs. Bush responded that being the president had nothing to do with it, because "George knows better."

Again, the crowd loved Bush's sharing of his personal story. Even if he had told it before, it still had a genuine feel. You could actually imagine it happening just that way because that's the thing about former president Bush. He may not be as savvy a speaker as Bill Clinton or as dynamic as some other big-name orators, but his human qualities come through and he connects with people on a very personal level. This is the essence of great communication, even for someone that has little natural ability.

In addition, Bush's candor ("I hated losing to Clinton in 1992") was another quality that made his presentation so effective. He also poked fun at the *New York Times* and the media in general, recounting a story about his son's visit to Yankee Stadium after 9/11 to throw out the first pitch of a big game. Bush senior joked that the newspaper described his son's pitch as "an apparent strike." Looking exasperated and shaking his head, Bush blurted out, "What the hell were they talking about? George's pitch was right down the middle." The crowd roared with laughter.

Finally, in his own self-deprecating way, the former president acknowledged that he was not the greatest public communicator and poked fun at both his and his son's much publicized past speaking mistakes. But he clearly showed that he gets it when responding to a question as to what it takes to be a really effective public communicator. "The key is to speak with conviction . . . to speak from your heart." And so he did. For that former president George Bush gets the award for being the most improved communicator . . . at least among former presidents.

Chapter 12

ANDREW CUOMO IS NO MARIO WHEN COMMUNICATING

This chapter was written after Andrew Cuomo dropped out of the New York governor's race seven days before the September 10, 2002, primary. One reason he quit in the eleventh hour was that by his own admission, he was trying to communicate "too many messages." At a press conference announcing that he was dropping out, Cuomo said, "It was like we had a new idea every day. We weren't focused enough on communicating a single message. Simplicity is very important in communication."

The lessons learned by Andy Cuomo have tremendous value for the rest of us. This is less about electoral politics than about people in leadership positions communicating effectively in an effort to get things done and rally the troops. We all do that, don't we? Campaigns are in many ways a microcosm of what we do every day in the workplace. We are like candidates communicating our ideas and approaches on a variety of issues, problems, and questions facing our organization. Our audiences vote on us and our message on a regular basis.

When you get up at a meeting and talk about a new project or initiative, you want your peers and bosses around you to support you. It's all about persuasion. The key to remember is that people aren't usually persuaded or moved (much less impressed) when we come up with a new idea or proposal every day. Sure, it shows you have a lot of imagination and energy, but the problem is that people can't keep track of your agenda. While they are just digesting your last idea, you are throwing a new one at them. It gets confusing.

When you communicate with the same enthusiasm and passion about more than a few messages, people begin to wonder what's *really* important to you. What are this guy's priorities? When they hear a laundry list of ideas coming from you, they begin to tune you out. When you are in a meeting with your boss or a potential client, the worst thing you can do is have a ton of points you want to make. Even if all your points are valid and you make a compelling case for each one, it's a poor communication strategy. People don't want to work that hard to keep up with you, so don't make them. It's a real turnoff.

Andy Cuomo was right about one thing. Simplicity is very important in communication. We're not talking about communicating simplistic ideas, but rather getting a single message across that is clear, concise, and credible. That message is your anchor. It grounds all of your communication in whatever "campaign" you are currently engaged in at work.

If you have lots of points or messages you plan to communicate in your next presentation—DON'T! Rather, ask yourself, "Of all these things I want to say, which one is the most important to me? Which message is the most important to my audience?" Try to answer these questions *before* you open your mouth. It takes discipline. It takes editing. And it takes introspection. Oh, yes, simplicity in communication is hard work, but it pays big dividends.

Chapter 13

COMMUNICATION RESOLUTIONS FOR A NEW YEAR

Making resolutions is a great way to start a new year, but any day is a good day for deciding to become a more effective communicator. How, you ask? One step at a time.

Today, resolve to:

- Be more honest and candid. We're not talking about being mean or going out of your way to be hurtful. Rather, this is about being more up front so you don't have to keep track of all those little white lies. For example, at work if you haven't returned a call or taken care of a certain project because you have been swamped, don't say, "Your message got lost," or "We're having problems with our computers." Instead, say, "I've really been swamped, and I haven't had a chance to get to the project but I'll have it to you by Friday."

- Become a more attentive listener. Next time you're in a meeting or conversation or any situation where you should be listening—concentrate more. Try to eliminate distractions and give yourself a reason to listen. Fight the urge to interrupt and finish other people's sentences. You'll be amazed at the results.

- Cut back on how often you interrupt people. The key is to practice identifying a reason to actually listen and then becoming just a bit more patient. Hear yourself interrupting in your head, but hold back from actually doing it. This is all about practicing a new behavior. Once you do it enough it starts to become second nature.

- Try a more passionate, attention-getting approach in your next presentation. Instead of starting like this: "Good afternoon. I'm here to talk to you about . . . ," begin with a provocative question or statement. The point is to give people a reason to listen and not come across like every other presenter they have ever heard.

- Get to the point faster and stop beating around the bush. If you hear yourself droning on, stop talking and ask yourself, "What was my point anyway?" Remember, when it comes to communication, brevity is usually the best policy.
- Speak in a more conversational tone. No one wants to hear a lecture or even a speech. Instead of a monologue, engage in a dialogue and promise to do less talking and more listening.
- Be clearer in the language you use. Instead of saying "I'll get it done ASAP" or the house "is not too far away," be specific. Say exactly when you'll get it done and how far away the house is. Most of us are unaware that the language we use often causes misunderstanding and miscommunication. Instead of blaming that on the other person, take more responsibility for how you communicate.
- Be more aware of your eye contact. Next time you are in a conversation or a meeting, concentrate with your eyes on the person who is speaking. Don't stare to the point of making people uncomfortable, but focus. It will help you to listen. If your eyes are darting all around the room and you are easily distracted, make note of it and the impact it is having on the other person.

The Power of Passion and
Connecting with Others

Chapter 14

NINE TOOLS OF THE COMPELLING COMMUNICATOR

The following are nine proven tools or techniques of a compelling communicator. (A list of ten would be way too predictable.) They can help you next time you have to make a presentation before any audience:

1. Use concrete, easy-to-understand examples that the audience can relate to. Examples are a powerful tool. They connect the audience to your main message. People tend to make presentations filled with facts, figures, statistics, charts, and graphs and ignore the simple example. People appreciate examples.

2. Use analogies. Like examples, analogies can help an audience better understand a complex system or procedure by comparing it to something that is more familiar to them.

3. Keep eye contact—steady, focused eye contact. One of the worst things people can do while presenting before a group is to not look people in the eye. I don't mean staring at people, I mean taking two or three seconds to look at a specific person in the audience. Talk to that person, connect with that person.

4. Repeat yourself. Repeat your main message several times throughout a presentation. You don't have to do it the same way every time, but make sure your message is crystal clear to the audience. Consider Martin Luther King's famous "I Have

a Dream" speech. He repeated the phrase "I have a dream" numerous times. Repetition is a powerful tool.

5. Use effective pauses. Don't you hate when people use "um," "ah," "like," or "you know" in their presentations? The reason they do this is because they're trying to get their words to catch up with their minds—or to get their minds in sync with their words. Don't be afraid to allow for silence. Think of silence in your presentation as "white space." I appreciate getting a written report with some "white space." I like print advertisements with "white space" around the message. The same holds true for a presentation. Pausing allows you to emphasize certain points and stay in sync.

6. Move your hands. Hand gestures are but one of many body language tools that should be incorporated into your presentations. You can use your hands to count—"I have *three* points I want to make." Or, to contrast the status quo with where you would like to be, put your left hand by your waist and your right hand up over your head. Use your hands to demonstrate contrast. Hand movements add to your presentation a lot.

7. Ask rhetorical questions. Rhetorical questions get your audience thinking. They don't put the audience on the spot by expecting them to blurt out an answer, but they do require the audience to think! Rhetorical questions keep your audience involved and engaged while keeping you in control.

8. Ask open-ended questions. Like rhetorical questions, open-ended questions keep your audience engaged and involved; however, they do require that the audience participate verbally in the presentation. The key to using good open-ended questions is to make sure the question requires more than a yes or no answer. Another effective tool here is to follow up the initial response to your open-ended question with an encourager like "Tell me more" or "Do you have an example?"

9. Close the deal. A good presentation has to tell people exactly what you want them to do when you are finished. Too often, people give great presentations and the audience doesn't know where to go from there. Do you want them to get back

to you by a certain date? Do you want them to change a current policy? Do you want them to just think about something you have told them? Bottom line is: Tell them exactly what you want them to do when you are finished.

Chapter 15

MEET SISTER MARIANNE MCCANN

For over twenty years, Sister Marianne McCann, principal of Paul VI High School in Haddon Township, New Jersey, was convinced that the only way she could deliver a presentation was to read it verbatim off index cards or a prepared text. Every time she would get up to speak she mistakenly thought that if she didn't have every word written down, she could never speak effectively in public. What pressure. She was so tied to her script that she even read it verbatim every morning when speaking over the intercom to her students.

I met Sister Marianne at a communication seminar I was conducting for Seton Hall University's doctoral program for school administrators. Every administrator was required to deliver a three- to five-minute presentation using only a bulleted outline with a few key words or phrases. The idea was to get them to connect with their audience on a more personal and human level. I told the administrators that in order to achieve this connection, you actually had to look at the audience and watch their reaction. You had to engage them, which you couldn't do if you were obsessed with your index cards or your written script. Most of the seminar participants reluctantly agreed to this approach. Not Sister Marianne.

She told me in no uncertain terms that she wouldn't, and in fact "couldn't," do it. I could see the fear in her face. Change can be really scary. I felt bad for her. Everyone did. Plus, I spent over a decade in Catholic school with nuns like Sister Marianne in charge. On numerous occasions I was reprimanded for inappropriate classroom behavior. I always seemed to be in trouble with the nuns. On a personal level I was a bit conflicted. How could I push Sister Marianne without having a classic case of Catholic guilt?

But I also knew that if she didn't seize this opportunity to break away from her obsessive connection to written script/cards, odds were she would never have the opportunity again. So I pushed.

Sister Marianne's presentation topic was a compelling one: "Why Being an Educator Really Matters." In coaching her I sensed great passion for the topic. She truly believed that being an educator was a noble profession. She also believed that being an educational administrator was God's work. I was convinced Sister Marianne could do the presentation in a compelling and dynamic fashion without reading it.

Sister Marianne finally agreed to try it using one index card with a simple outline. Surprisingly, when she presented in front of her thirty colleagues, she didn't even look at her card. While she started slowly, once she tapped into her passion Sister Marianne built up a powerful head of steam. Her voice became animated. Her body language supported everything she was saying. She moved from behind the podium and got much closer to her audience. She used personal anecdotes and examples to support her message and she used the names of audience members (other educators) whom she knew felt as she did. She was smiling, and so was her audience, who knew what she had gone through to present in this new way. When she finished, she got a standing ovation. It changed the way Sister Marianne McCann would speak in public from that day forward.

Chapter 16

WHAT'S YOUR CQ? (WE'RE TALKING COMMUNICATION QUOTIENT)

It's time to get serious about your CQ—"Communication Quotient." What good is it if you are really smart but can't get your point across and connect with others? The most successful professionals are those with the best relationships, not always with the greatest intellect. But always, they are the best communicators.

In order to reach you potential as a communicator, you have to ask yourself some tough questions concerning how you see your communication style as well as how those around you see it. Further, you need to follow up and make a commitment to improve your communication weaknesses. So here we go. It is time to take a communication inventory:

- List three adjectives that best describe your communication style when dealing with those around you at work. Is your style significantly different at home? If so, how?
- List three adjectives that you think those closest to you would use to describe your communication style.
- Ask others. Select at least six, but no more than ten, people you work closely with (or family members) and ask them the following question: "What three adjectives would you use to describe my communication style?" Also ask respondents to provide specific examples to explain their answers. Then ask those same people to identify the communication skill that you most need to improve. If you want to provide confidentiality, ask them to type their responses and put them, unsigned, in a box.
- Compare your answers to those around you. Where are the similarities? Where are the greatest differences? What was the biggest surprise or disappointment to you?
- Given these results, what one area do you need to improve in the way you communicate (or don't communicate) with those around you? For example, "I need to be a more patient

listener." Or, "I would like to speak up more at meetings when I really have something to contribute."

- Time for action. Identify one specific situation where you can and, more importantly, you will, practice getting better. What specific action are you going to take that will produce this improvement? For example, say you want to work on your listening skills: "In this week's staff meeting, I am going to work harder to concentrate on what others say and follow up with specific questions. I'm also going to fight the urge to interrupt just because a thought comes into my mind."

- Finally, how *specifically* are you going to monitor or evaluate your communication progress in this area? Consider this suggestion. Three months from now, go back and ask those same people how they think you are doing. Ask, "On a scale from one to five, to what degree to you believe my communication skills regarding XYZ have improved in the last three months?" One is virtually no progress, and five means you are hitting a home run. Also ask respondents to provide at least one concrete example to support their answer regardless of whether they give you a one or a five.

Sounds like a lot of work, right? Well, becoming a great communicator doesn't happen overnight and it's not easy. But the payoff is huge. Go ahead, take the test. What do you have to lose?

Chapter 17

"BUT I HAVE MORE SLIDES . . ."

Timing is everything—as recently demonstrated at a national drug awareness and prevention conference. A large crowd of nearly 200 gathered to find out more about how they could protect their children and others from the scourge of drugs. This was a highly motivated audience.

A panel of three teenagers, ages fifteen, sixteen, and eighteen, had the audience enthralled as they told their individual stories of drug use beginning as early as age nine and moving quickly from marijuana to heroine. Their stories were personal and painful. Their struggle to stay clean and sober resonated in a deep and emotional way. Later, a member of Congress gave a brief five-minute speech about what he and his colleagues were doing to respond to the drug problem. He was concise, to the point, and was well received by the audience.

Because the conference had a very busy agenda, each speaker was given a certain amount of time. One of those speakers, a much-acclaimed researcher who had spent years analyzing drug use among teens, was asked to give a ten-minute PowerPoint presentation. The researcher's first few slides were interesting even though she spoke in a monotone voice with little passion. However, within minutes it was painfully clear that she was losing the audience. Her numbers, displayed in a myriad of graphs and charts, were beginning to blur and confuse. The energized audience was being brought down by the dreaded data dump.

Ironically, the researcher was specifically asked by conference organizers not to use "too many numbers or slides." After about ten minutes she announced she had only a few more slides. About twenty slides into the presentation, something had to be done. Conference organizers asked the moderator to get a message to the speaker. By now, many in the audience were shuffling in their seats, checking their Blackberries, talking on cell phones, and looking at their watches. I could have sworn a few of them were actually sleeping.

Finally the moderator walked up to the speaker and quietly whispered, "Doctor, you are going to have to wrap it up." The speaker looked stunned and responded, "But I have more slides." Then she said to the audience, "I'm being told I have to wrap it up, but I'm just getting to what I really wanted to say."

What? How could she just be getting to what she wanted to say twenty minutes into the presentation? A good communicator *leads* with the main message. You don't wait until you've lost your audience and any semblance of momentum before you say "what you really want to say." The speaker fast-forwarded through her PowerPoint slides until she got to her last one. She hurried her final comments, unable to conclude with a powerful take-away or "call to action." She simply ended because she was being forced to get off the stage.

The communication moral is clear. If you are given ten minutes to speak, plan to do eight with a two-minute cushion. Don't try to cram twenty-five minutes of statistics, charts, and graphs into an already crowded agenda. Talking faster won't help, either. Your audience can handle only so much information at one time. Great communication is not about telling your audience about how much research you've done. It's about sharing information that the audience cares about and can use. This highly credentialed researcher, who had spent years mastering this complex subject of drug addiction, had spent no time trying to master the art of connecting with her audience in a meaningful way. For that, she gets an F.

Chapter 18

PLANNING A CONFERENCE? NO DETAIL IS TOO SMALL

You've heard them before—those incredibly long, overly detailed, and frankly boring presentations that cause otherwise dynamic events to grind to a halt. Follow these steps to run a dynamic, interactive, goal-oriented event:

- Establish exactly what you want to accomplish in the event. What are your two or three main goals? What are the "take-aways" you want participants to leave with? Once you have answered these questions, you are ready to move forward.
- Keep things interactive and dynamic. You can't allow speakers to come in one after the other to provide their own "unique" expert perspective to the audience. Inevitably, after the second or third speaker, the audience begins to lose it.
- Make sure all speakers understand that they are part of a larger conversation. Their perspective is important, but it is not the only one. Let them know up front exactly how much time they have. Further, discourage them from making a

"canned presentation" and limit the number of PowerPoint presentations.

- Bring in a professional moderator who is an expert at drawing out your speakers as well as your audience. Even if the staff of your organization is competent in many areas, the ability to effectively facilitate and lead a conference is rare. Invest a few dollars in doing this. It will be worth it.
- Once you have the facilitator in place, use him or her. Make it clear to your invited speakers that they will be part of a "facilitated conversation." Tell them that they will have the opportunity to share their perspective, but it is essential that they do it in an interactive and dynamic fashion. You can have as many as a dozen or more speakers at one conference, but none should seem isolated from the others.
- All speakers should be pressed to share their views. However, they should be pushed by the facilitator to keep their comments relevant to the conference's larger goals. If not, the conference will be all over the place, and it will be impossible to tie things together at the end.
- Never end any event without having the moderator publicly state what has been agreed to by event participants. It is essential that people can point to exactly what has been accomplished through their participation. One of the worst feelings comes from spending an entire day at a conference and then walking away exhausted without a clear sense of what had been accomplished.

How do you handle speakers who are resistant to your approach? Level with them. It's worth making the effort up front and communicating in a direct fashion about what you are trying to accomplish. No matter how important these people may be, no conference organizer should turn over an event to a single speaker. If a speaker resists, you should seriously consider withdrawing your invitation.

Dynamic presentations don't happen by accident. They take planning, preparation, and persistence. Yet, the payoff is more than worth it in satisfied customers who are likely to return the next time you invite them to another event.

Chapter 19

WHY ARE WE HERE?

Jim is a long-time manager who recently attended a conference in which a corporate executive talked about his company's newest product. The executive's presentation was very detailed and very long. It was filled with lots of facts and figures, and it proceeded in a logical and orderly fashion. But it was REALLY boring.

At the end of the presentation, the unenthusiastic audience applauded politely. There were no questions. The speaker then handed out a brochure about his company's new product, saying he wanted to provide "additional information." The information in the brochure seemed awfully familiar to Jim. He quickly realized that virtually every point raised in the brochure was discussed at length in the presentation he had just heard.

Jim asked himself, "Why did I have to spend a half an hour listening to this guy tell me everything that was in a brochure he could have sent to me?" When Jim told me about this experience, he wondered out loud if the speaker ever thought about how his presentation would be different from the written material he handed out after the presentation?

Brochures, manuals, PowerPoint—you name it. If all the speaker is going to do is repeat what is on a slide or in a brochure, why do we have to be here? That is the issue. Anytime you have the opportunity to communicate face-to-face, you have to ask yourself, "What do I bring to this presentation?" Too often, a speaker goes on "automatic pilot" and spouts out exactly what is in his or her script. When this occurs, many things happen and few of them are good:

- The audience is turned off. They know you are following a script and feel you have no connection to them. They are bored.
- You are bored, too. You are reading the same material in every presentation. No deviation. Nothing to mix it up. How could you expect your audience to get excited when you have no passion or enthusiasm?

- You've just wasted a lot of time and missed an important opportunity to connect with people beyond simply disseminating information.

The next time you are asked to give a presentation, consider a few questions:

- What can I personally add to the prepared material I am giving to my audience?
- What personal or profound experience can I share that drives my message home?
- Is there a recent event common to the group that will help them feel more engaged and involved in the presentation?
- Is there an example or anecdote that brings my PowerPoint slide or brochure to life?
- Finally, why am I here giving this presentation and what right do I have to ask these people to sit through it?

As Roger Ailes, CEO of the Fox News Channel and former media consultant to President George H. W. Bush, once said regarding presentations, "You are the Message." If they don't believe in you, what makes you think they are going to believe in what you say? Those who ask and answer the questions listed above reap big dividends. Those who don't are just going through the motions and paying a hefty price.

Chapter 20

Q = A + 1

Bridging is a communication technique that involves making a transition from a challenging or controversial question back to your main message. It can help you confidently handle any question—hostile or otherwise—whether you're facing a reporter as tough as Sam Donaldson or an audience member looking to take you on in a question-and-answer session after a speech or presentation.

One of the most effective bridging techniques has been developed by Human Resources consultant Don Teff. It's called the "Q = A + 1" formula. Teff says that when asked a question (Q) you should reply briefly and directly with an answer (A). Then you should add a specific point (+ 1) that goes directly to the agenda you want to communicate. Roger Ailes, media maven and former communications consultant for Ronald Reagan, uses an excellent example of a Q = A + 1 formula in his book *You Are the Message: Getting What You Want by Being Who You Are.*

Ailes cites one of his clients, a member of Congress who was asked by a reporter, "You were pressured by the big chemical companies not to introduce that legislation, weren't you?"

The congressman answered, "I met with everyone involved in this issue, including the environmentalists, the consumer groups, and the companies." That was the brief answer (A).

Then he added the + 1. "Based on these discussions, all the parties agreed that the industry would set new standards rather than Congress passing a law."

The key here was to give a very brief response to a potentially hostile question rather than getting caught up in a detailed protracted answer or debate. Once that is accomplished, the savvy communicator bridges or makes a transition back to his or her agenda or message. Some people, particularly politicians looking to avoid giving any direct response, bridge from a question directly to their message without providing the slightest response. This is risky, particularly if the reporter or audience member has asked a legitimate question. Your credibility is on the line.

A while back, former New York governor Mario Cuomo was pressured very hard during an interview by ABC's Sam Donaldson with the following question: "Governor, isn't it true that another group of Catholics has gone to the Pope to ask him to excommunicate you because of your pro-choice position on abortion?"

Without losing his cool or missing a beat Mario Cuomo responded, "Sam, I hate to be so precise about the facts. I know it gets in the way of discussion. But no group of Catholics has gone to the Pope. My position on abortion is absolutely theologically sound. But you know Sam, we should forget all the argumentation about *Roe v. Wade.* The Supreme Court will decide that. What we should do is get all the pro-lifers and all the pro-choicers into a room and get them to figure out how we can help women avoid unintended pregnancies and do it in accordance with their conscience."

Donaldson persisted, saying, "But governor, doesn't the Pope want to excommunicate you?"

Cuomo leaned forward and said, "The Pope has never spoken on Mario Cuomo's position and Lord knows the leader of the whole world's Catholic Church has more important things to think about than the baggy-eyed governor of New York who's in trouble with his budget."

Score one for Mario Cuomo. Sam Donaldson had nowhere to go. The key is that Cuomo anticipated hostile questioning on the subject of abortion. His strategy no matter what he was asked on the subject was to briefly respond and bridge back to his message, which in this case was talking about how to help women avoid unintended pregnancies (which no one could be against) and that the Pope was too important to be thinking about Mario Cuomo.

Such communication savvy doesn't happen by accident or overnight. It's part of a plan that is designed and practiced again and again. $Q = A + 1$. It makes sense, doesn't it?

Chapter 21

WHAT WE REALLY WANT FROM OUR LEADERS

January is the time of year when leaders in both the public and private sectors get ready to make important presentations to very important audiences. Governors of state and the President of the United States deliver annual addresses at the beginning of the year. CEOs and other top executives have been working feverishly with their communication teams to talk to shareholders and employees about the "big picture." No easy feat during these extremely difficult times.

But while communicators in charge spend countless hours gathering data, verifying facts, developing PowerPoint slides, and prettying up lots of charts and graphs, one critical question often gets overlooked. *What does my audience really want from me?* Here are some things that most members of your audience will be listening for:

The facts. Most people want you to be honest with them. They are looking for candor about the difficult challenges and problems your organization faces. Of course they'd rather not hear it, but what's the alternative? Lying, deception? That's what the executives at Enron did and look at the price that company paid.

Reason to hope. While people appreciate your candor and honesty, they also need you to tell them that the glass is half-full, not half-empty. People are looking for the silver lining because if things are so bad and there is no hope, why should they keep plugging away? It's what the management of the New York Jets did after they got crushed by the Raiders in a critical late-season game. Sure they lost, and on some level "failed," but the owners and coaches congratulated the players on turning what was a dismal season into something very positive to build upon next year.

Passion. Let your audience know what you feel, not simply what you think. This is all about passion. People want to know what is in your heart as well as what is in your head. Disclose a little bit of yourself. Most people appreciate and respect that. If your presentation is all about the facts, why not just send out an e-mail and save time for everyone?

Challenge. More than forty years ago, President John F. Kennedy asked Americans to consider not just what their country could do for them, but what they could do for their country. That message still resonates today. People want to be part of the solution and want to give more of themselves. Great leaders find a way to tap into that desire.

Direction. Once you've connected with people on an emotional and personal level, your responsibility is to give them practical tools and advice. This will provide direction for them to channel their efforts.

Clarity. Audiences want to know, "What's the point?" Your audience wants to be able to follow what you are saying without racking their brains. State your message up front, state it again, and conclude by stating it one more time with feeling.

Brevity. Too many of these annual addresses last nearly an hour or more. Way too long! You know you can do it in half the time. Try editing and prioritizing. Your audience will love you for it.

The bottom line is that more leaders need to spend more time thinking about what their audience wants as opposed to focusing on showing off how much they know or think they should know. A little bit of empathy goes a long way here. Remember, people don't care about what you say until they know how much you care.

Chapter 22

MOST GREAT SPEAKERS ARE MADE NOT BORN

People seem to believe that being a great public speaker is something you're born with. He or she is a "natural born speaker" I hear people say. They see speakers like John F. Kennedy, Bill Clinton, Ronald Reagan, Elizabeth Dole, and Dr. Martin Luther King and say all these communicators were given a gift that the rest of us mere mortals don't possess. I don't buy it.

In the vast majority of cases, great communicators have worked hard to get to be where they are. It's just that the rest of us never get to see the effort it took to be that good.

Consider former president Bill Clinton. Like the rest of us, Clinton made some horrible speeches early in his career. Consider his nominating speech for Michael Dukakis at the 1988 Democratic National Convention. It was terrible. Clinton rambled for fifty-seven minutes. He had lost his audience after the first ten minutes and didn't know how to get them back. He was wed to his script.

The crowd kept booing. They begged him to stop, but Clinton lacked the experience and the know-how to cut his losses. By the time he uttered the words "in conclusion," he received a mock standing ovation from over 20,000 loyalists in his own party. By any standard, his speech was a bomb that had missed its mark. He was laughed at and ridiculed as an embarrassing public speaker who was in no way presidential material.

After that fiasco Bill Clinton made a commitment to learn everything he could about being a great public speaker. For the next decade, he worked on such skills as speaking off key bullet points and making more direct eye contact with his audience. He started using more examples and anecdotes to support his message and became more conversational and less preachy. He also learned to edit.

Also consider the late Robert F. Kennedy. At the time of his death, Kennedy was considered a marvelous public speaker who was comfortable in virtually any setting. He could touch people with his passion and emotion. But the Kennedy of 1968 was not the Kennedy of just a few years before. According to many accounts, RFK was deathly afraid of speaking in public. In early interviews he was known to stumble and stutter. He admitted to being extremely nervous when having to speak. In fact, he believed his brother Jack was the natural born speaker in the family. Once he was appointed attorney general in 1961, Bobby Kennedy tirelessly worked to improve the way he communicated in public. He learned what it took to connect with his audience on a deeper, more visceral level. Like Clinton, it was a question of practice, patience, and persistence.

Remember Elizabeth Dole's innovative and dynamic Oprah-like presentation at a recent Republican National Convention? Mrs. Dole moved beyond the podium and strolled through the audience, talking with and touching people in a relaxed, informal, and highly conversational fashion. On television, it looked like she was born to play this role.

In fact, Elizabeth Dole had worked on that speech in countless dress rehearsals in smaller venues. She honed her skills by making numerous mistakes and by making a commitment to improve her effort. By the time she spoke to the nation on national TV, she was ready for prime time. Again, all we see is the final product and consider Mrs. Dole another one of those "natural born speakers." Like I said, I don't buy it.

Chapter 23

MARIO CUOMO SPEAKS FROM THE HEART

Mario Cuomo is undoubtedly one of the most effective public speakers of our time. As former governor of New York and a much-sought-after motivational speaker, Cuomo has studied other great orators and has worked hard to master the art of connecting with and persuading people.

In 1984, along with millions of others, I watched Cuomo deliver a spellbinding speech at the Democratic National Convention. That speech is considered by many to be one of the greatest political convention speeches ever.

In a recent interview with Cuomo at the New Jersey Performing Arts Center, I asked him what the essence of powerful and persuasive communication really is, be it in politics or business. Cuomo hesitated, shook his head, and said, "I don't know, but I know some of the ingredients." Cuomo talked about other great communicators like Martin Luther King, who had a "profound belief, an idea that is worthwhile and a real commitment to that idea." Cuomo says that the idea or belief you are talking about doesn't have to be complicated, but you have to be sincere: "There are very few people who can give a really effective speech or presentation and not believe what they are saying. You have to be a gifted fraud, and I don't know many."

Cuomo says the greatest speech he ever heard was Dr. King's "I Have a Dream" speech. "King was committed to the truth of freedom for his people, fairness for his people and for all people." Cuomo is dead on here. Nearly thirty years later, that speech by Martin Luther King resonates and touches us in so many ways.

It's been said in this space before, but speaking more from your heart rather than from your head is usually more effective. Intellect has its place but great communication goes deeper than that. It is much more personal and human, bordering on spiritual. Cuomo offers this perspective: "The speech I gave in '84, both Walter Cronkite and David Brinkley said it was the greatest reaction to a speech in a hall they have ever heard. And it was a tremendous reaction." Yet, Cuomo says the speech wasn't that special. He said he didn't use any special words or "magical poetry." Cuomo was convinced that what made the speech so effective were the ideas embodied in it: "We have a country here that is the most powerful country in the world and you have more and more people on that shining hill. But there are people in the gutter where the glitter doesn't shine and we are ignoring those people."

Mario Cuomo says it is not about poetry, but I disagree. Much of his masterful communication ability is because he is so poetic. Yet, there is a danger in holding up Mario Cuomo or Martin Luther King as paragons of excellent communication. Most of us don't see ourselves in that light. We are convinced that they are gifted, somehow anointed by a greater force or spirit with this "natural ability." But if we do that we miss the main point. You don't have to be Cuomo or King to be an effective public speaker. The challenge is to push ourselves outside our comfort zone and have faith in what we believe.

Consider Mario Cuomo's advice on this issue in talking about the overwhelming reaction he received back in '84: "Yes, it was passionate, but it was a profound idea and people knew I believed it. And so what happened is that I was opening the book of their life. They were reading their own thoughts. It wasn't me. They didn't know who Mario 'Cucomo' was. They still don't. So I know the necessary ingredient. You have to be talking about something profoundly significant and you have to mean it."

Like I said, it is ultimately about speaking from the heart.

Chapter 24

RUDY IS A "HIT" AT THE YOGI CLASSIC

Former New York mayor Rudy Giuliani is a complicated guy. He's a terrific public communicator. Much of the nation saw that in the summer of 2004 when he addressed the Republican National Convention in a powerful and engaging speech. While I disagree with his handling of the much-publicized Bernie Kerik affair surrounding his nomination as head of Homeland Security, Giuliani is still great on his feet, as I witnessed at the Annual Yogi Berra Celebrity Golf Classic, where he gave a dinner speech to a crowd of several hundred of Yogi's friends and admirers.

Giuliani is considered by many to be a top-notch platform speaker, particularly on the subject of leadership. Yet, watching him speak at the Yogi event crystallized why he connects with his audience on a variety of levels.

- Giuliani didn't read from any prepared text. He didn't even use notes. But he wasn't shooting from the hip.
- He had a clear and compelling message, which was that great athletes and others who excel perform with "grace under pressure." He repeated this theme and broke it down with concrete examples, utilizing several people in the audience including Yogi as well as former Yankees greats Goose Gossage and Craig Nettles.
- Every time Giuliani mentioned these guys by name, the crowd responded with applause. He understood the importance of highlighting people who are familiar to your audience in order to make a personal connection. In Giuliani's book, entitled *Leadership,* he states, "The point is not to alter your message depending on the audience, but to present it so that it could be understood by whomever you are addressing."
- Giuliani is an animated storyteller. He shared with the audience a story about the time he went to a Yankees playoff game in the 1980s. He gave just enough details to paint a vivid picture of him sitting "two rows from the top." (Rudy said, "I wasn't always mayor, you know," referring to his less than desirable seats). He talked about what happened in the game and how the Yankees won dramatically by "performing with grace under pressure." Great storytellers don't get bogged down with the minor details, but use vivid language and have a memorable point to their story.
- While Giuliani is funny on his feet, he is not a joke teller. Telling jokes is risky and should be left to professional comedians. However, Rudy's humor is quick and seizes the moment.

For example, at one point Giuliani referred to the value of "Yogi's philosophy of life." After a moment of confused silence, someone yelled out "what philosophy?" Without missing a beat, Giuliani laughed and responded, "Well, whatever it is." The crowd roared. Giuliani immediately understood the humor in referring to Yogi Berra as having a "philosophy." We're talking about the same guy who became famous for saying, "When you see the fork in the road, take it."

- Physical presence and command of his body language. Giuliani immediately moved from behind the podium using a hand-held microphone. Even though he had only a few feet on either side of the podium, he used his space well. Further, when he referred to Goose Gossage, who was sitting in front of him, he placed his hand on Gossage's shoulder. The ability to know when and how to actually touch an audience member can be a powerful communication tool that few speakers understand.

- Finally, Giuliani's dinner speech lasted no longer than seven minutes. He understood the importance of brevity and being concise. He also knew that even though it was a friendly crowd, the longer he talked, the greater the risk of losing them. Less IS usually more—just one of the many communication tips and tools Rudy Giuliani knows and the rest of us should remember the next time we have to stand and deliver.

Chapter 25

"PRESIDENTIAL" PRESENTATION MATTERS A LOT

Electing a president is about a lot more than politics and policy. In an age of instant, nonstop news coverage and an electronic media obsessed with the public "gaffes" of those who seek to lead the nation, electing a president is largely about presentation, appearance, likability, and communication skills.

In fact, a front-page *Star-Ledger* story written by Scott Orr entitled, "It's True: White Teeth Can Lead to the White House," examined the smiles of the men running for president in 2004. Superficial? Maybe, but then again don't we all form impressions and make decisions based in large part on how people present themselves and make us feel about ourselves? Do I like you? This is as true in a presidential campaign as it is in the corporate boardroom, hiring a manager at your local ShopRite, or deciding if you want to say "yes" when asked on a date.

Beyond issues and ideology, many Americans select a president based on the following criteria:

- We want a straight talker. You don't have to be the greatest orator in the world for us to like you. Of course, you have to be competent and coherent, but what is most important is that candidates don't engage in using inside-the-Beltway Washington-speak that only political and policy junkies can understand.
- We like brevity. Why do candidates' speeches have to go on for so long? Why does the State of the Union last nearly an hour? The only people who can keep our attention for that long are extraordinary public communicators in the Dr. Martin Luther King mode. And since most mere mortals can't do that, just cut it down. We'd rather you give a five- or a ten-minute speech that hits the mark as opposed to droning on, saying "in conclusion" five separate times.
- We like presidential candidates who admit their mistakes quickly. Most people are pretty forgiving, as long as they know you take full responsibility for your actions, are sorry for anyone you have hurt, and are committed to doing better. There are only a few really egregious mistakes we won't forgive a candidate for.
- We like candidates who are confident in not just what they say, but how they say it. It's important for those who seek to be president to have body language that is consistent with their words. We don't like our presidents to sweat in public, nor to

nervously fidget when pressed. Again, selecting a president isn't that different from selecting a leader of your team at work or buying from a particular salesperson.

- Speaking of white teeth, we like candidates who can smile easily as opposed to when their media gurus tell them to. We like presidential candidates who can poke fun at themselves in a speech on a talk show without coming across as a buffoon. Simply put, we like our candidates to be comfortable with themselves.
- We like presidential candidates who can speak off the cuff or from a bullet-point outline as opposed to having to read every speech from a written script or, worse, from a TelePrompTer.
- We want a president with passion and conviction. We need to know that you believe in what you are saying. But, a candidate can communication these things without screaming at the top of his lungs (a lesson Howard Dean learned a little too late).
- We like presidential candidates who are positive and optimistic and communicate a clear vision of where they want to take the country. Conversely, we don't like candidates who constantly bash their opponent as if they are the biggest creep in the world. Comparing yourself to your opponent is one thing, trashing him or her is another.
- We like candidates who can laugh at themselves—who don't feel a need to come off as perfect. If you fall or stumble, laugh about it. If you misspeak, it's no big deal, unless you act like it never happened.

Yes, presidential presentation matters an awful lot.

Chapter 26

DEAN'S SCREAM ENDED HIS DREAM

Watching Howard Dean deliver his concession speech after the Iowa Caucuses in the 2004 Democratic Presidential primary underscored the point that often it's not just what you say that counts, but how you say it. This chapter is not about politics or the presidential race, but rather illustrates why those in a position to communicate publicly must be aware of their demeanor and its impact on others.

While Dean was a distant third in Iowa, he wanted to communicate the message to his supporters that things were looking up and it was not time to quit. No problem with that. His execution, however, was another story. Jacket off, shirt sleeves rolled up, and microphone in hand, there was Howard Dean screaming at the top of his lungs, "We have just begun to fight. We have just begun to fight. And we are going to fight and fight and fight."

He then continued to scream about where he was going to fight, naming various states holding presidential primaries: "We're going to New Hampshire, South Carolina, New York. . . ." As he did this, his face was contorted and his body language was anything but under control. At the end of his speech he let out a perplexing howl that sounded like a weightlifter who had just finished breaking a world record and was now screaming in celebration.

No one should criticize Howard Dean or anyone else for wanting to pump up the troops. Passion clearly has its place. But, if in the effort to do it you come off as angry and enraged, bad things often happen. This is particularly true when the position you attempt to hold is so important. Whether we are talking presidents of the United States, or the CEO of a major company, demeanor and communication style matter a lot.

As soon as I saw Dean's speech I knew he had a problem. There was little doubt television networks would replay this part of his speech over and over again, cementing this image of the screaming candidate in our minds as well as in our psyches.

Skip Cimino, senior vice president for public affairs at Schoor DePalma, is the former commissioner of the New Jersey Department of

Personnel. Cimino has spent years evaluating employees' professional potential based on their communication skills and says there is a big difference between being enthusiastic and being "over the edge" in your communication. Says Cimino, "What a speaker, be it a presidential candidate or the manager of a workplace team, needs to convey to people is a confidence in his message without being shrill. In his speech, Howard Dean lacked a real sense of understanding that his message was being communicated not just to a group of supporters, but to the entire country via television."

Any speaker, but particularly one in such a high-visibility position, must understand who their audience is and how that audience is likely to perceive their message and the delivery of it. So here's the deal. If you want to be enthusiastic in your communication, that's great, just do it without screaming. Screaming has no place in campaigns or in business. It also has no place with teachers attempting to motivate students or parents trying to change a child's behavior. The only place screaming may work is on the football field, and I'm not so sure about that. Just know that even though we are sometimes tempted to scream and yell at the top of our lungs, when we actually do it, we pay a hefty price. For if we are too loud for too long, our audience may not hear what we are saying because they are so turned off by our approach.

Chapter 27

WHY KERRY DIDN'T CONNECT

Massachusetts senator John Kerry lost the 2004 presidential race for a lot of reasons. One of the biggest was that he never really "made the connection" with many Americans. Kerry was smart and knew the issues. He was a better debater than President Bush and he spoke the English language more effectively than the president. Still, Kerry never really connected on an emotional and personal level. He just wasn't that likable.

Here are the reasons Kerry missed the mark:

- Kerry rarely showed human emotion and vulnerability. He seemed so focused on attacking President Bush that you didn't get to see who he really was as a person. Most people need to see you in this way, particularly if you are not the incumbent. Kerry never gave people the chance to get to know him. He never really opened up. What's ironic is that he was at his best in his "concession" speech the day after the election. He seemed genuine and not at all in "campaign mode." Clearly he was disappointed, but he seemed at peace. He spoke in a softer, more conversational and accessible style. One wonders why he couldn't do it sooner.

- Most of Kerry's speeches were just too long. He got into this terrible habit while pontificating on the floor of the U.S. Senate. It wasn't all that effective there, but who was going to tell him? But it was worse on the campaign trail. Kerry never mastered the art of brevity. He always seemed to use more words than he needed.

- Kerry didn't smile enough, and when he did it seemed a bit forced or staged. In order to truly connect, people need to see you have the ability to smile easily in a variety of situations. Senator Kerry just seemed too serious, if not somber, too much of the time.

- Teresa didn't help. Teresa Heinz Kerry is a smart, articulate, and very independent woman. Not to mention obscenely rich. But it didn't help her husband's candidacy when she cursed at a reporter, talked about their sex life (who cares?), and then committed the cardinal sin of criticizing Laura Bush, saying she has never had a "real job." We like Laura Bush. She is a terrific first lady and in fact spent many years as an educator and librarian and then as a mother. Those sound like real jobs to me. Teresa Heinz Kerry never really connected, and that made it only harder for her husband. Some people say her accent didn't help. I say her accent only became an issue because she wasn't that likable in the first place. If we liked her more, her accent would have been irrelevant. Most people, regardless of ideology or politics, were turned off by Teresa.

- Kerry never communicated clearly and aggressively when he was attacked on the Swift Boat issue. Kerry was a genuine war hero in Vietnam (Bush clearly wasn't), but he never seemed comfortable talking about that experience in a way that connected with most voters. He made things worse at the Democratic National Convention when he began his speech surrounded by supporting Vietnam vets and then saluting and declaring, "I'm John Kerry and I'm reporting for duty." That was a bad canned one-liner and it only invited the attacks from Republicans and some not-so-sympathetic veterans. When Kerry was attacked, he didn't know how to respond. He tried to play the victim, but that didn't work. He waited too long to make his case. Kerry should have found a way to talk about his Vietnam experience without dumb one-liners and staged visuals. As a war hero, he never should have been vulnerable on this issue. Yet he was, because he couldn't figure out how to connect. And perhaps because he spoke of his service "too much," at the expense of laying out proposals.

- Bad photo opportunities communicating the wrong messages. What was Kerry doing dressed up in a hunting outfit carrying a rifle right before the election? Was this supposed to communicate that he was pro guns? Pro hunting? Or just that he was willing to dress up in any ridiculous outfit to appeal to a certain constituency? In most cases, dressing up or having your picture taken in unrealistic situations (think Michael Dukakis in 1988 with an oversized army helmet covering his eyes as he rode in a tank attempting to show he was "tough on defense") is both bad politics and bad communication. The moral here is that most candidates including Kerry (and President Bush, when he played fighter pilot in that dopey "mission accomplished" debacle) seem oblivious to the fact that most people are turned off by all this. I say, don't dress up or down (Al Gore in 2000 wearing "earth tones") or have your picture taken in a campaign doing something you wouldn't do in real life. It's a simple rule that gets broken all the time.

Since Kerry didn't connect in the way he should have, George Bush is our president again.

Leadership

Chapter 28

"YOU LIKE ME . . . YOU REALLY LIKE ME!"

"You like me . . . you really like me." Those were the unforgettable words of actress Sally Field when she won the Academy Award for Best Actress in 1985. Like Fields, we all have a strong need to be liked. Yet, when it comes to real leadership, the kind that moves organizations forward when faced with difficult challenges and obstacles, the desire to be popular and overly friendly can get in the way.

If you are a manager, supervisor, or chief executive, there are countless situations where you must make decisions that will make some people uncomfortable. In fact, if you are really doing your job, there are times when people are going to be downright angry with you. In his book *The Leadership Secrets of Colin Powell*, Oren Harari quotes the secretary of state on the need to sometimes get people angry for doing what a leader needs to do. "Being responsible sometimes means pissing people off."

Of course, being social, relaxed, humorous, and, yes, friendly, are important aspects of being a good team player in the workplace. Yet, the problem arises when people in leadership positions at all levels of an organization confuse the workplace with the rest of their lives.

Consider the expression, "If you want to be liked, get a dog." Sure, it's a bit extreme, but there is something to be said about that way of thinking. Consider how difficult it would be to assertively challenge or reprimand a colleague whom you consider a friend. Further, with conflicts that arise every day in our professional lives, a real leader must make tough decisions.

With that said, following are some tips for remaining focused on your responsibilities as a leader without getting caught up in a popularity contest:

- Seek opportunities to make tough decisions so it's clear to everyone in the organization that it is more important for you to be a leader than to be universally well liked. If budgets need to be cut, make a conscious decision to use productivity and effectiveness as the measuring stick instead of the personal relationships.

- Set a goal and work backward from there. If you want to meet a specific deadline on a specific project, for example, press employees to keep their eye on the ball until that goal is reached. Limit the water cooler banter while working on the project and when the job is done, reward employees with some time for celebration.

- Keep socializing to specific situations (such as during lunch or after work). Making the office a prime social gathering place could encourage laid-back attitudes and blur the lines of work and play. Inviting your employees to be social with you only at certain times sends a message that it's okay to chat and be friendly with the boss, but that once you get into your work area, it's time to get down to business.

- If you have to review an employee, use that time to be honest and constructive in your criticism. Don't hold back. To do so is cheating the employee and the organization. You may have a longstanding relationship, but the employee needs to know that your ultimate concern is with his or her performance and the team's success.

- Don't try to be a stand-up comic. There is a fine line between being funny and being crude and obnoxious. Use caution when joking with employees. It is up to you as the leader to maintain a level of professionalism within the organization without being a stiff.

Simply put, if you are uncomfortable about occasionally making your teammates in the workplace feel uncomfortable, rethink whether you really want to step up and lead.

Chapter 29

ATTITUDE IS JUST ABOUT EVERYTHING

You hear it all the time: "Jim has a really bad attitude and it's killing his career," or "Mary's negativity brings down the whole team." It's so true that the attitude a person brings into the workplace has a tremendous impact on everyone's effectiveness. How's your attitude? Do you see a "problem" as an insurmountable crisis or as an opportunity to challenge yourself as a leader as well as your team to be creative and cohesive?

Your attitude can give you a huge competitive edge or it can kill your chances of succeeding before you even start. In fact, the Stanford Research Institute found that the money you make in any endeavor is determined 12.5 percent by knowledge and 87.5 percent on your ability to deal with people—in other words, your attitude. Many people mistakenly believe that their attitude is dictated almost entirely by the circumstance they face. Think again. Consider the people you know who "have it all" yet still have miserable attitudes. Conversely, we see even more people who overcome great physical or personal tragedies to accomplish great things and make a positive impact on others.

Consider Denny Chipollini, whose leg was severed below the knee in an auto accident. Instead of asking "Why me?" and packing it in, Denny decided to run marathons (with one prosthetic leg) in order to raise money for an organization he founded called Generation Hope—dedicated to helping inspire and educate kids and adults to overcome adversity. Their slogan? "No excuses and no limits."

Or what about Julie Goldman, who in her early thirties was stricken with terminal cancer? Instead of pulling the covers over her head and hiding from the world, Julie decided to dedicate the remaining few years of her life to teaching physicians dealing with terminal patients to become more empathetic and compassionate communicators. She appeared on television, published extensively, and gave countless speeches and seminars on the subject. Even though Julie is gone, her impact continues to be felt.

Julie Goldman and Denny Chipollini are examples of great leaders, and their leadership abilities are largely based on having a positive

"I can make a difference" attitude. Consider some things that you can do to have a more positive attitude at work that will pay big dividends:

- Read an inspiring book. For example, try *Tuesdays with Morrie,* the story of someone who turned a chronic illness into an opportunity to teach, inspire, and connect with others.
- Rent a motivational movie, such as *Rudy,* that demonstrates that you can do anything you put your heart into.
- Make a commitment to help someone else. Helping other people has a tremendously positive impact on your attitude. It can make you feel relevant and give you a sense of purpose.
- Finally, when you are feeling that your attitude isn't what it should be, look around at seemingly less-fortunate individuals whose lives and attitudes epitomize what you would like to become.

In the end, it is all about your attitude.

Chapter 30

TAKE THE LEADERSHIP TEST

In a recent boardroom episode of *The Apprentice,* the contestants for another Donald Trump "dream job" were asked by Trump if they considered themselves to be good leaders. The answers were predictable. "Of course I'm a good leader." "People like and respect me." "I give clear direction." "Yes, I AM a leader." We've all heard these things before.

Most folks do consider themselves to be good leaders. But leadership is not an absolute thing. It is not black and white. Some days we are better leaders than on others. In fact, we may demonstrate superior leadership on one specific task and a short time later fall on our face when up against another. That's why the really great leaders are constantly engaged in self-examination and finding ways to get better.

With this in mind, consider the following questions that will help you measure your individual leadership ability. Rather than answer just yes or no, use the following scoring system: four is "always," three is "most of the time," two is "rarely," and one is "never."

- I give honest feedback to my workplace colleagues, whether I like them personally or not, because it is in the best interest of our team.
- I am open to feedback and constructive criticism from others at work regarding my performance and behavior, even if I am not enamored by the source.
- I take risks and propose new and innovative ideas in meetings when our team seems stuck on a particular issue or challenge. Simply put—I speak up when my team needs me.
- When things do go wrong and mistakes are made, I step up and take responsibility for my actions.
- When things go right, I aggressively seek to identify others who deserve credit, even slightly overstating their contribution because I know how important it is that professionals feel they are making a contribution. In the process, I even understate my role, because drawing attention to myself may not necessarily help the team.
- I give clear, concise direction as to what needs to be done and why. I state our goal as well as the consequences for failure in ways that leave little doubt as to what the real picture is.
- I seek to monitor and coach colleagues and team members because I see their professional development and improvement as critical to our workplace's overall success.
- I stay calm in a crisis, even if there is a strong part of me that does feel anxious, nervous, uncomfortable, or even angry. I understand that how I react to this type of situation communicates a powerful message to those around me about how all of us should act when things don't go exactly as planned.
- If someone (including a top leader in my organization) did something that was either ethically or morally wrong in order to gain a competitive advantage, I would step up and make it clear how I felt, even if it jeopardized my professional status.

- When two colleagues or direct reports are engaged in an unhealthy or unproductive argument, or are simply not working well together, I take the initiative to sit them down and identify tangible ways for them to work together more effectively, even if it is uncomfortable and a genuine pain in the neck.

Forty is the highest score you can get on this little evaluation. What's your score? What does that say about your goals to strengthen your leadership skills?

Chapter 31

GREAT LEADERS MAKE GREAT TEACHERS

In the recent edition of *Fast Company* magazine, Chuck Salter makes a powerful connection between the fields of leadership and teaching in his article "Attention Class: 16 Ways to Be a Smarter Teacher." All types of teachers, from those in the classroom to CEOs of big and small corporations, weighed in on the issue of leadership. Consider the following tips to help you be the best teacher/leader you can be:

- View yourself as a "guide" for your students or employees. Instead of seeing yourself as an expert who holds on to important information, share what you know. The focus is not on you as the smartest person in the class or on the team, but rather on the people who need to better understand what needs to be done.
- Allow the people on your team to take risks. "Learning takes vulnerability" according to Michelle Foreman, the 2001 National Teacher of the Year. Foreman says it can be scary for students as well as for people in the workforce to acknowledge in public what they don't know. The key is for them to know they can trust the teacher or leader not to make them look bad. Sounds so logical. Then why do so many teachers

and leaders go out of their way to make their students and employees look bad?

- Have passion for what you teach as well as for those you are trying to teach and learn from. Passion can't be faked. Students, as well as employees, know whether you care or not. Great teachers and leaders teach from the heart.

- Communicate with your employees. When you break it down, teaching and leading largely come down to communication. People need to understand what you are trying to accomplish and why. This is particularly true of organizations undergoing significant change. Beyond employees, partners, and customers, all shareholders need to understand where the organization is going and how they are invested in the outcome. That's about communication and teaching.

- Don't be afraid to say "I don't know" when you don't. Being a good teacher doesn't mean you have to be an expert on every issue or question. When people know you respect them enough to be honest about what you don't know, they tend to appreciate you more. The beauty is that teachers and students can sometimes learn the answers together. That's what great teamwork is all about.

- Don't do data dumps. As a leader, it is important that you don't simply pass out information. Your goal should be to get people to think for themselves and ask the right questions. They can't do that if leaders and teachers are spoon-feeding them the so-called right answers. Consider the adage, "Give a man a fish, he'll eat for a day. Teach him how to fish and he'll eat for a lifetime."

- Finally, be a great listener. Like leadership, teaching must be a two-way street. It's a dialogue, not a monologue. Learn to ask engaging, open-ended questions. If you don't get an answer right away, relax. Allow for the silence. Wait patiently for a response. Silence and the thinking that hopefully goes with it can be a powerful part of the teaching process.

Great teachers, like great leaders, see themselves as students who never stop learning.

Chapter 32

HANK KEIRSEY STEPS UP

There have been countless books written about essential leadership traits or characteristics; few mention that sometimes being a great leader involves taking the blame for the actions of someone on your team. It's about sacrificing your personal and professional success for something larger. A lot of people talk the talk, but in a moment of truth retired Lt. Col. Hank Keirsey walked the walk.

In 1999 a West Point aviation captain by the name of Dan Dent created a PowerPoint slide involving inappropriate homosexual humor. The slide, which was meant as an inside joke, was accidentally circulated. The incident was immediately brought to the military powers that be. Dan Dent, who had two small children and another on the way, was in deep trouble. Lieutenant Colonel Keirsey then decided to go to his superiors and take full responsibility for the incident as Dent's commanding officer.

Keirsey says he did it because it was the right thing to do. He also felt that as a military veteran he would probably get a slap on the wrist, as opposed to Captain Dent, who would face much worse. Except that's not what happened. Despite twenty-four years of dedicated military service and an exemplary record of training thousands of young cadets in leadership at West Point, Lt. Col. Hank Keirsey was thrown out—discharged—with the following explanation: "LTC Keirsey . . . has created and fostered an environment in military training that is antithetical to Army values, professional standards, and the development of cadets into officers of character." The West Point community was stunned.

Recently I asked Keirsey about the incident, which is profiled in the book *Absolutely American* written by David Lipsky. Says Keirsey, "There are two kinds of leaders. There's the guy that puts his arms around his subordinates and creates an environment and climate of trust that a guy can operate in. This leader stands behind his people in times of crisis and stress. Then, there is the other guy that is immediately looking for a scapegoat when something happens. This guy snuffs the life out of an organization."

In *Absolutely American,* Hank Keirsey is seen as an exceptional leader, a role model for those who aspire to have others follow them when things really get rough. Hank Keirsey took a bullet for one of his team members, the kind of bullet that ended a distinguished career in an instant. Dan Dent may have made the mistake, but Keirsey held himself personally responsible for this captain's actions.

Consider how rare this kind of leadership is in business. How many high-profile figures are quick to blame subordinates for things that go wrong? Scapegoating has become an art form in today's workplace.

Former president Harry Truman once said, "The buck stops here." Yet, it often seems that a more appropriate adage for certain professionals today might be, "The buck stops with anyone but me." When I asked Hank Keirsey about this phenomenon, he offered this perspective: "I think we have a weakness with people in corporate America fully understanding what leadership is. Most of our corporate executives understand management and checking on things. They understand there are systems of managing information and projects and setting suspensions and dates. However, when it comes to walking into a room and inspiring a number of people saying, 'I'm not here for the pay or the benefits. I am here because I don't want to disappoint my team.' This is something we need to develop in our leaders today."

This column often talks about the importance of communication and the power of the spoken word when it comes to leadership. But in this instance, as Hank Keirsey clearly demonstrated, sometimes actions do speak a lot louder than words.

Chapter 33

GREAT LEADERS AREN'T ALWAYS IN THE TOP SPOT

There are certain characteristics that great leaders share. Here is a collection of traits to emulate and some insights about leadership from my readers.

Great leaders:

Have "unrealistic" expectations as to what is possible. Consider how Dr. Martin Luther King's "unrealistic" expectations dramatically changed the course of history. Great leaders don't simply make incremental change or improvement, but rather strive for goals and objectives that most others are threatened by. The key is to motivate team members to believe that together they can accomplish great things. Whether it's Mother Teresa, Gandhi, Bill Gates, or Dr. King, our world is shaped by "unrealistic" expectations.

Aren't necessarily at the top of the organizational chart. Their leadership is not defined by title or position in the organization. The fact is, there are many CEOs and others in key positions who on paper exhibit few, if any, characteristics of great leadership. I've known many great leaders who have had a great impact on their organization despite the fact that they did not have the title, position, or status. Leadership is as much an attitude and philosophy as anything else.

Understand that different situations may require different leadership styles. When people say they have a democratic leadership style my question is, "Would you use that same style if there was a fire or some emergency that required you to give clear and undebatable direction?" The fact is, while someone may have a general leadership style, there will be situations that arise that require a leader to adapt a different approach. Leaders who refuse to do so will hurt themselves and their teams.

Are committed to their personal and professional growth. Great leaders never stop learning. The leaders who think they have all the answers are in big trouble. While leaders must be good teachers, they must also be students and have a desire for new knowledge and insight. Great leaders are committed to reaching their potential, which requires an open mind and a desire to grow.

In that spirit of learning let's consider the comments of a few readers on the subject of great leadership.

One reader, who has worked in public service for thirty years, says an important characteristic of a good leader is that he or she "delegates appropriate responsibility and with it the authority needed to maximize customer services. When a leader entrusts an employee with the responsibility and authority to do a job, it results in not only a more efficient service but also maximizes the employee's self-esteem."

Great stuff, reader. Delegating responsibility is a great way to boost the morale of the entire team.

Another reader believes a great leader is someone who listens attentively to other's opinions. "Too many of us," he says, "are poor listeners. Poor leaders tend to listen to their own voice rather than the valuable opinions of their team members."

This person is right. Listening is one of a leader's most important skills. Of course it's important for a leader to be able to make powerful presentations. But if I had to choose between a leader being a great public speaker and a great listener, I'd go with the latter. Leaders cannot lead without working overtime on understanding what team members are saying or not saying. Listening is not easy, but it pays huge dividends.

Finally, I will leave you with a few characteristics of a great leader sent to me by a reader: "A great leader is someone who understands the need for effective two-way communication from the executive level to the front-line staff; has a visceral, unflinching way of demonstrating to employees how to deal with change; has a clear sense of what his or her principles are and how important it is to never contradict them."

Chapter 34

WHEN DELEGATING, DON'T UNDO

One of the hardest aspects of a leader's job is delegating. Yet, it's a must if a leader wants to see the forest for the trees or the "big picture." Some of the reasons we find it hard to delegate is because we fear:

- we will lose control
- we may not get credit
- we may be outshone by a subordinate
- others will not do the job exactly the way we would do it

Clearly, fear has a lot to do with our delegation problems. It takes faith in people and in ourselves. It takes coaching and open-minded communication. And it also requires that we give up some authority.

One of the cardinal rules in the delegation game is that once authority is given, it should rarely if ever be taken back. Consider an incident involving the New York Yankees that is less about baseball and a lot more about leadership and communication.

Owner George Steinbrenner and manager Joe Torre were equally perplexed as to what to do about the poor performance of a $32-million pitcher named Jose Contreras. Steinbrenner, who is known as "The Boss," told Torre that it was the manager's call on Contreras. Torre then told the pitcher that he was being sent to the Yankees's minor league team in Columbus to work out some of his problems. Immediately following, Steinbrenner overruled Torre, insisting that Contreras report to Tampa to work with one of Steinbrenner's pitching gurus.

Joe Torre was livid. His entire philosophy of managing is based on building and maintaining trust. We're talking about a manager with an impeccable track record whose reputation is based on his candid and consistent communication with team members.

"My problem with this whole thing," said Torre, "is that I sat with this young man and it turns out I'm the liar. That I'm not crazy about. I always am as honest as possible and I pride myself on that. . . . I know my place and I know my job, but don't tell me I can make a decision and then tell me it's not my decision and not have it be that way."

Like I said, this isn't about baseball. This kind of thing happens every day in organizational life. Responsibilities are delegated with the implied authority necessary, and then all of a sudden the rug gets pulled out. When this happens, the results are often ugly. Relationships are strained. The reputation of the leader delegating has been damaged, and his ability to delegate in the future seriously hurt. The message is sent that full delegation will occur only if the boss agrees with the decision. Bad stuff. Plus, the employee's authority is undermined and bad precedents are set. What happens in the future if a player (or an employee) disagrees with the manager's decision? Does he simply appeal it to a higher authority knowing that decisions can be undone as they have in the past?

Interestingly, Steinbrenner is supposedly a student of great leadership. But he clearly broke one of its most important and basic rules. Never delegate authority and then undo it simply because you have a different point of view.

One final thought: If you must undo what you have delegated, a real leader steps up and communicates personally and directly. Ironically, George Steinbrenner delegated to one of his assistants the job of delivering the bad news to Joe Torre. In my opinion, Steinbrenner compounded the problem.

Chapter 35

THE CHALLENGE OF CHANGE

New York City is trying to implement a major restructuring of the public schools. In New Jersey, political leaders and child advocates rail about the need to overhaul the state's child welfare system that some say is responsible for the recent deaths of two children in foster care. Countless corporations, nonprofits, and institutions of higher learning say they need to *change* in order to survive.

Yet, when it comes to real, enduring change, talking about it is one thing, doing it is quite another. The obstacles and challenges to successful change are considerable. One of the biggest reasons change efforts fail is because so-called leaders refuse to acknowledge that these obstacles and challenges exist, much less deal with them directly.

With this in mind, consider some of the keys to successfully managing change in your organization:

- Make it crystal clear that there is an urgent need for change and that the status quo is unacceptable. Too often, organizational leaders propose change for the sake of change. That won't do. There must be a compelling rationale that is communicated in tangible terms; otherwise, buying in will be difficult at best.

- Explain in specific understandable language what the tangible benefits of this change will be. People need to see what the payoff is for investing in the change process. Don't assume they know, because they probably don't.

- Don't sugarcoat what it is going to take to implement this change, including the sacrifices as well as any pain that might be involved. If you do, employees could resent the change and you as the change agent for being less than honest with them.

- Facilitate an ongoing and highly focused dialogue with key shareholders through meetings and seminars, as well as through printed and electronic communication.

- While being clear on the reasons for change, remain flexible and open to feedback regarding new and different approaches to implementing change. There is nothing worse than change agents who are rigid and closed-minded about anything other than their own ideas.

- Celebrate and recognize any success or accomplishment associated with the change effort, no matter how small. People need to see progress in order to buy in to the change. Remember, everyone wants to be part of a winning team.

- When confronted with opposition to the change, see it as an opportunity. Don't duck hard questions. You will be perceived as someone who isn't truly convinced that the change really makes sense. If employees don't believe you believe in it, you can forget about them coming on board.

- Understand that any real change takes time. While a sense of urgency is important, so is having patience. It may sound like a contradiction, but it's not. Try to avoid becoming frustrated because some on your employees don't get it or refuse to get it. The status quo can be very attractive. People have a hard time moving outside their comfort zone. Try to be empathetic and understanding about this.

- Finally, avoid the temptation to pull out the hammer and force compliance. This rarely if ever works over the long haul. Too often, managers get caught up in the desire to have a change effort appear to be successful. That shouldn't be your goal. Rather, you should work toward getting genuine buy-in to the change so your organization can reap the benefits the change was designed to produce.

Chapter 36

WITH FEEDBACK, ACCENTUATE THE POSITIVE

Being a great leader is largely about being a coach and mentor, yet much of coaching and mentoring comes down to knowing how to give constructive feedback to team members. So, let's take a look at some methods of giving feedback in ways that won't make you look like you're criticizing or chastising:

- When giving feedback, be as specific as possible. An example might be: "Mary, you did a great job on the Jones report. Let's take it a step further. I noticed that you didn't go into great detail on what you think our options are. Next time, make concrete recommendations that evaluate the costs and the risks." The key is to give people information that they can do something with. Conversely, if you say, "Way to go on the Jones report, Mary," that's okay to a point, but sooner or later Mary needs to know *exactly* what she did right and what she needs to do to improve her performance and contribute to the team in the future.

- Avoid judgmental comments. For example, "Mary, you need to be more enthusiastic about working here. Your casual attitude is starting to affect your work." First of all, what exactly does "enthusiastic" mean? That's a very subjective word. Further, how exactly is Mary's lack of enthusiasm affecting her work performance? The problem is that the leader/coach has said nothing that Mary can use to improve her performance.

Further, such "you need to . . ." statements cause many people to become unnecessarily defensive.

- Give feedback face to face. Sure, e-mail, faxes, and phone messages can supplement your coaching efforts, but the most powerful and effective feedback is usually in person. You can read the body language and attempt to interpret the reaction to your feedback. It's hard to do that when you are communicating via technology.

- Go out of your way to catch people doing things *right* as opposed to catching them doing things *wrong*. People often think coaching is about saying "don't do this" or "why did you do this?" A more constructive approach is to recognize and acknowledge positive work efforts, thereby reinforcing them. For example, "Jim, I want you to know that I really like the way you handled the Jones project. You were calm and reasonable when some others might have overreacted. Good job."

- Keep a positive attitude. If someone on your team is falling behind or has missed a deadline, you might ask, "What obstacles or issues are getting in the way of you meeting the goals we agreed on?" The key here is to frame the feedback in a positive fashion as opposed to assigning blame or fault.

- Give feedback as quickly as you can. Too often, leaders and managers wait too long to talk to an employee about something they are concerned about. The problem is that the feedback is often lost. This is particularly true when trying to give positive feedback. Recognize people's efforts *immediately.* However, according to Marty Brounstein, the author of *Coaching and Mentoring for Dummies:* "When giving negative feedback you may want to apply a different timeline: ASAR (As Soon As Reasonable/Ready)." According to Brounstein, sometimes leaders need some time to cool off after an incident and get their thoughts together before dealing with the situation.

- Finally, when giving feedback, work hard at being a great listener. When you ask a team member a question, give them the respect of listening and thinking about their response. Great coaches are great listeners.

Chapter 37

THE SEVEN DEADLY SINS OF LEADERSHIP

Leadership is a complicated craft. There have been countless books and scholarly articles written on the subject. There are leadership gurus like Tom Peters and America's mayor, Rudy Giuliani. Yet, when you talk to most leaders, you find out that a lot of what they've learned about leadership has come through the mistakes they or those around them have made. Simply put, leadership involves a lot of trial and error. With that in mind, consider the following seven deadly sins of leadership:

1. Micromanaging. Attention to detail is one thing, but hovering over your people once you've given them an assignment is quite another. Too many managers are convinced that no one can do a job better than they can, so they hold on way too tight. This is a big mistake because while you are micromanaging your people, lots of strategic opportunities are being missed. Plus, your people lose motivation.

2. Surrounding yourself with "yes" men and women. Sure, it makes your ego feel good to have people kiss up to you, but this has a terrible effect on the decisions you make. Leaders need to be challenged and sometimes criticized by those around them. It's healthy and normal. Someone has to tell the emperor he has no clothes on.

3. Poor listening. Too many managers don't listen because they think they have all the answers or simply lack the patience to listen. Big mistake. When your people come to realize that you are not listening to them, they begin to shut down and stop making suggestions and being straight with you. If you think you have all the answers, think again. No one does.

4. Not acknowledging or thanking your people. Some people in top positions are either too self-absorbed or just assume their people know that they are doing a good job. Leaders who don't get into the habit of saying "nice job" to their people run the risk of alienating productive employees. No matter

how talented or secure, everyone needs to be thanked and acknowledged. Leaders who ignore this pay a heavy price.

5. Not growing and learning. Some managers stop reading, researching, going to seminars, and refuse to be open to new ideas or ways of doing things. This can be out of laziness or once again because they think they have all the answers. Leaders who stop growing and learning get stale very quickly. There is always a new approach or idea that leaders should know about. Being closed-minded is very dangerous for any leader.

6. Not being candid with employees. People know times are tough and sometimes leaders have to make very tough decisions like laying people off, forgoing bonuses, and cutting back on perks. When leaders refuse to be up-front with their employees or sugarcoat the painful facts, they lose credibility. Being a leader is not a popularity contest. In the end, a leader must have the respect of his or her people, even if they are not happy with some of your decisions.

7. Running really boring and uninspiring meetings. Come on, you know it's true. If your boss runs a meeting that is rambling and unfocused, and he or she does all the talking and nothing is accomplished, how do you feel? Running effective meetings is one of a leader's most important jobs. To take that responsibility lightly is a big mistake.

Chapter 38

GINNY BAUER LEADS WITH HER HEART

By any standard, Virginia Bauer is an exceptional leader. What is particularly interesting about her is that she didn't come to leadership by any traditional route. Virginia lost her husband, David, who worked for Cantor Fitzgerald, in the World Trade Center attack on September 11,

2001. Years back, Ginny (as she likes to be called) worked for Merrill Lynch. For the next seventeen years, though, she dedicated most of her life to her three children. As was the case for thousands of people in the New York City area, 9/11 changed everything.

But Ginny felt she had no choice but to step up and lead. While dealing with her own grief and loss she began organizing the widows and family members of 9/11 victims. There was a narrow window of opportunity from September 11 to the end of 2001 to enact federal tax relief legislation for surviving family members. She testified before Congress and communicated very directly with U.S. senators as well as White House officials about the need to get this legislation signed quickly. She went on countless television programs to persuade the public that sympathy wasn't enough and that action was essential. In January 2002, along with her three children, Ginny stood next to President Bush while he signed the tax relief legislation benefiting 9/11 family members.

Because of those efforts, then- New Jersey governor Jim McGreevey asked Bauer to serve as executive director of the New Jersey Lottery, where she led the lottery effort in the state with the same passion and enthusiasm that she showed after 9/11. Later, Ginny Bauer was promoted to the position of secretary of commerce in New Jersey and is currently receiving accolades for her leadership style in this position. For Ginny, the key to leadership comes down to a few simple but powerful tools:

- Get to know your team. Says Ginny, "At least once or twice a day I make it a point to walk around and talk with the 150 people in our office. I simply say hi, wave, or stop to have a one-on-one conversation. It creates a stronger sense of unity. For the lottery to be successful, I need to know my people. If I can help to make their jobs better, success will follow."
- Connect with your audience in order to persuade them. "I let them know that I care about them." What Ginny Bauer understands is that people have to know you care in order for them to care about what you have to say. Again, a simple but powerful leadership tool.
- Don't try to copy someone else's leadership style. Ginny says, "What has always helped me is being myself. If you are who you are and don't try to pretend to be something you are not,

that is the key. Be comfortable in your own skin." But she warns, knowing yourself isn't enough. You also have to "know your material and know your subject."

- Know that you don't need to have all the answers. "I'm not afraid to ask questions. Sometimes a leader tries to fudge things and pretend he knows all. Some leaders feel that by asking a question, they will lose respect. But you really gain respect by asking honest questions and the wealth of information I've gained from my employees and those around me has helped me make some really great decisions."

The lesson of Ginny Bauer is pretty clear. Leaders come in all shapes and sizes and they don't all have Harvard MBAs. Often, people are put into positions because of unforeseen circumstances (sometimes tragedies) and find out what's really inside of themselves. One might say, these people lead from the heart. It's about an intense desire to make a difference in the lives of others. There are millions of Ginny Bauers out there that lead in this inspiring way on a daily basis. We just don't know their names.

Chapter 39

RUDY'S RULES OF LEADERSHIP

Rudy Giuliani has written a new book called *Leadership*. In it, the guy who has become known as "America's Mayor" as a result of September 11 offers a range of tips and tools for any leader dealing with any circumstance or situation. Much of what Giuliani offers is not necessarily new or earth-shattering, but rather reinforces some things that most managers know but too often don't practice. Here are some of Rudy's rules of leadership:

- Sweat the small stuff. Giuliani says that leaders who micromanage get a bad rap. He argues that it is critically important to understand how something works so you can evaluate the performance of those who work for you, but also to ask probing questions of the process. He also says getting involved in certain details communicates to your team that you really care. However, be careful not to take this "small stuff" approach to an extreme. This denies the leader the opportunity to see the forest for the trees.

- Meetings matter a lot. Giuliani swears by the daily 8 A.M. meeting he conducted as mayor of New York. He says it wasn't just the idea of meeting itself that mattered, but how those meetings were conducted. Giuliani set the tone in those meetings in which each manager was expected to report on relevant information and to respond to difficult challenges and questions.
- Leaders have to control their emotions under pressure. Giuliani says there is a big difference between having a "concerned" attitude during a crisis and expressing panic. Panic only makes things worse, while concern communicates seriousness. Giuliani says it was this approach of not letting himself become paralyzed regardless of the situation that helped him lead effectively in the aftermath of September 11.
- Actively seek input and advice from others with more experience and expertise than you. Giuliani says that too often leaders think that reaching out for help communicates weakness or vulnerability when in fact quite the opposite is true. The key is for the leader to be secure enough to admit that he or she doesn't have all the answers (no one does) and enthusiastically receive contributions from others.
- Great leaders are not afraid to make really tough decisions. Making the right choices is the most important part of leadership, says Giuliani. He argues that many CEOs and other top players in corporate America engage in procrastination, which has the potential of paralyzing an organization.
- Great leaders don't hide behind other people. They are willing to take responsibility for their decisions and choices and not allow those around them to filter valuable information and take the hit when things go wrong. This is all about accountability. If a leader is held accountable for his actions, it makes it

clear to other team members that they, too, will be held to the same standard.

- Leadership has a lot to do with the language you use. Giuliani says it took him years to understand that as a leader, he needed to communicate using words that would connect with people on a deeper level. The point is not to alter your message depending upon your audience, but to present it so that it can be understood by whomever you are addressing.
- Don't be a bully when you are in charge. To his credit, Giuliani acknowledges that he was somewhat of a bully as mayor, imposing his will through intimidation. He says that over time he learned that such a strategy created unnecessary enemies and obstacles.
- Finally, Giuliani argues that great leaders never stop learning, especially about themselves and what they need to improve.

Chapter 40

GREAT FACILITATION PAYS BIG DIVIDENDS

Many people in business are asked to lead or facilitate meetings, conferences, or forums. Being asked to do this is often an honor and sometimes turns out to be an excellent opportunity to show your stuff and make a meaningful difference in your organization. Unfortunately, just as often, you might fall flat on your face.

The funny thing about facilitating is that most managers, supervisors, and others don't have a clue how to do it. Facilitating is not the same as giving a speech on a specific subject. You don't even have to be the expert on whatever issue is being explored. Great facilitation, regardless of the venue, is about creating an open, relaxed, but most important, interactive environment in which all participants feel comfortable asking questions and expressing their views.

Unfortunately, the ability to facilitate is not something people are born with. It is not a God-given gift. Rather, it is something that people have to learn through coaching and practice. It is something that corporations and other organizations must be committed to if they want their meetings, seminars, workshops, or employee conferences to be successful. In that spirit, next time you are asked to facilitate, consider these helpful tips:

- Set the tone for the conversation right up-front. Make it clear exactly what the group is attempting to accomplish. Say it early and often so that there is no confusion.
- When you ask questions, ask them of a specific person for a specific reason. Make sure you understand who is in the room and why he or she is there. One of the biggest mistakes that facilitators make is to throw a generic question out to no one in particular and then they wonder why they can't get the dialogue going.
- Be proactive. If someone says something that is especially provocative or controversial, ask someone else to comment on what has just been said. Your goal is to have the most honest, meaningful dialogue possible about an important but often unresolved issue. Shying away from sensitive but relevant subjects is a mistake. The more your audience sees that you are comfortable with straight talk, the more comfortable they will be.
- If a participant is going on too long and won't get off of the soapbox, move closer to that person. That's right, move away from the podium. As you move closer to the person, he or she will begin to get the hint that it is time to wrap up. If not, politely but directly say something like, "Bob, we appreciate your points but how are they connected to the problem or issue we are here to talk about?" This will let Bob and everyone else know that we are not here for people to make long-winded speeches just so they can hear themselves talk. We're here to solve a problem and move forward.
- Paraphrase what you think you've just heard so you that when the participants leave, they all take away the same message. The facilitator's job is to clarify and focus everyone.

- Finally, great facilitators understand that they aren't really the star or the focal point of the meeting or event. The facilitator's job is to draw others out. Therefore, great facilitators understand that they shouldn't be doing most of the talking. They should be asking succinct, open-ended, but very direct questions.

The bottom line is that effective facilitators can have a tremendous impact on the productivity and success of an organization. But this doesn't happen by accident.

Chapter 41

JACK WELCH LEADS "FROM THE GUT"

Former GE chief Jack Welch has written a great book called *Jack: Straight from the Gut.* It's an honest, straightforward, and highly practical work that focuses largely on issues of leadership and communication. One chapter that is particularly compelling is entitled "What This CEO Thing Is All About." In it, Welch says there is no pat formula to being a CEO, because everyone does it differently and there is no one right or wrong way to go about it. Welch admits he has no magic formula, but does offer some valuable ideas as to what worked for him and might work for you.

Welch says that the first thing you need is integrity. "Establishing integrity and never wavering from it supported everything I did through good and bad times. People may not have agreed with me on every issue—and I may not have been right all the time—but they always knew they were getting it straight and honest."

Welch is right on here. We would hope that most leaders lead with integrity, yet do you really believe that people who consistently give it to you "straight and honest" in the world of business are the norm?

Welch is a big believer in informality in the workplace, arguing that "bureaucracy strangles; informality liberates." He says that creating an informal atmosphere is a competitive advantage, while a bureaucracy can be an ultimate insulator. Welch says, "Informality isn't about first names, unassigned parking spaces or casual clothing. It's so much deeper. It's about making sure everybody counts—and everyone knows they count. Titles don't matter. . . . Passion, chemistry and idea-flow from any level at any place are what matter."

Welch also says that passion is a must for any CEO or leader. "If there is one characteristic all winners share, it's that they care more than anyone else. No detail is too small to sweat or too large to dream." Welch's definition of passionate leadership doesn't necessarily mean being boisterous or loud. Passion comes in all shapes and sizes and takes many different forms. Ultimately, passion can come from only one place: "From deep inside," as Welch puts it.

This kind of passion drives an organization to achieve things most team members never dreamed possible. Passionate leaders get people to look inside themselves and give more, create more, and risk more. What can be more important than that?

Now let's talk communication. Welch says that whenever he had an idea or message he wanted to drive into the organization, he could "never say it enough." In his book, he says he would often repeat a message or theme over and over at every meeting and review for years "until I would almost gag on the words." Some felt that Welch would often go too far in this area. Yet he says he often went "over the top" in order to get hundreds of thousands of people behind a particular idea. Bottom line, you cannot truly lead without being an exceptional communicator committed to constantly finding new and different ways to get your message across to sometimes skeptical and wary audiences.

As for having a business strategy, Jack Welch says this comes second to having great people in the right jobs. "I sat for years looking at promising strategies that never delivered results. We had great plans for ultrasound [at GE], but we could never make it happen until we found the perfect person with ultrasound in his veins."

Think about it. Inevitably, the workplace success we recognize is not about organizational charts or voluminous strategic plans. It's about people who make a difference at every level of an organization. Apparently, GE's former top guy Jack Welch understood that—and a lot more.

Chapter 42

BILL PARCELLS A LEADERSHIP GURU? NOT SO FAST

In the late 1990s, the *Harvard Business Review* did a profile on one of the most successful, "confrontational" leaders in America, former Jets and Giants coach Bill Parcells, who currently coaches the Dallas Cowboys. While Parcells succeeded on the football field, winning two Super Bowls with the Giants, he is a much sought-after motivational speaker in the world of business. Those who pay him big bucks to share his wisdom must believe that leading a football team isn't that much different from leading a business enterprise.

With that in mind, consider Bill Parcells's philosophy when it comes to the power of confrontation. The coach says, "don't wait to earn your leadership; impose it." He argues that getting the most out of people requires that you "apply pressure—that's the only thing that any of us really responds to." According to Parcells, the best way to apply pressure to people is confrontation, even though it can get "very intense, very emotional."

Parcells says that leaders, be it on the football field or in the world of business, make a big mistake when they avoid confrontation because their players or people don't like conflict. He says he actually "relishes confrontation, not because it makes me feel powerful but because it provides an opportunity to get things straight with people."

Who can argue with Bill Parcells's success on the football field? But one must question whether his confrontational approach would really work in any other environment. Let's be clear. As a leader, Parcells has a history of screaming at and berating players when they made mistakes. He embarrassed them on national television. He threatened them with losing their jobs to other players who were willing to work harder and smarter. He questioned his players' manhood for not being tough enough to do what it took to win. And like a lot of other sports coaches, he used profanity every step of the way.

Like I said, who can argue with two Super Bowl victories and an impressive won-loss record? But I'm just not convinced that the Bill Parcells's philosophy ("without confrontation, you're not going to change the way they think and act") translates off the football field. How many really talented, committed people will simply walk away and refuse to work under such leadership? Further, did Parcells really help each player reach his potential? How many did he turn off and demotivate because most talented people won't be ridiculed in public or private by their boss? How many players would have responded more favorably to being listened to as opposed to being yelled at and confronted?

Again, is the measure of a leader purely about the bottom line? Wins and losses? Profit and loss? Would these same confrontational techniques be criticized if Parcells hadn't won those two Super Bowls? Then again, some argue those Super Bowls wouldn't have been won if he didn't use such a confrontational, "in your face" style. This isn't about football or sports; it's about leadership, communication, and motivating others in the workplace. Ask yourself: would you want to work for a confrontational leader like Bill Parcells even if his approach greatly increased your organization's chances of success?

Organizational Life

Chapter 43

MICROMANAGING DOESN'T AVOID MISTAKES

There is a fine line between paying attention to important details and obsessively micromanaging an operation. Like you, I know countless people in the workplace who engage in this kind of micromanaging—no job or responsibility is too small for them. It's not enough to assign a project to a particular staff person. They have to know where that person is on the project every step of the way. Micromanagers second-guess and hover over their employees' shoulders. They are so caught up with the minutia of their operation that they don't have the time or the ability to see the bigger picture as well as new opportunities on the horizon.

To be fair, I can understand why people micromanage. The fact is, I have been guilty of it with certain people in certain situations. For most people, this need comes from the combination of their own insecurity, a lack of trust in others' ability, and an unhealthy desire to control everything that goes on.

Recently I got a letter from Mary Johnson, who complained that her boss was a compulsive micromanager. According to Mary, "He doesn't seek or welcome my input before or during a project. When he does meet with me, he critiques almost every detail of my work. His behavior makes me feel like he doesn't trust my judgment or value my skills. I have no sense of being part of a team nor do I have ownership in my work."

The irony is that I bet Mary's boss thinks he is actually doing a good job by showing his *interest* in Mary's work. Odds are, he is oblivious to how unhappy she is and to the fact that, as she told me in her letter, she is "actively job hunting."

The first step in dealing with the problem of micromanaging is to get leaders to acknowledge what they are doing and the negative impact it has on others. The old adage, "If you want a job done right, you have to do it yourself" doesn't work when you are part of a larger team that's supposed to be supporting each other and working together.

If you micromanage more than you know you should, it's time to accept the fact that you can't do it all yourself. Further, you *shouldn't* do it all yourself. Imagine being on a basketball team in which one player dribbled the ball up-court, took the shot, followed up his own rebound, shot again, never passed to anyone else, and then gave himself his own high-five. What fun would that be? Even if the team won occasionally, over the long haul, failure is guaranteed.

The same thing is true in the world of business. If one person, regardless of how smart or talented, refuses to delegate and share responsibility and authority, other team players will begin to lose interest and stop making a meaningful contribution. My advice to micromanagers is to delegate a little bit at a time. Ask yourself what assignment or project could be handled by someone else, thereby allowing you to do something that only you can do. There are simply too many tasks that need to be accomplished for you to do them all.

Further, avoid the blame game. I know from personal experience, every time I engage in finger-pointing and blaming (because secretly I'm thinking I could have done the job better), only bad things happen. Accept the fact that, occasionally, things won't go exactly as planned. No matter how hard you try, or how many hours you work, no leader, manager, or supervisor can control everything that goes on around him or her.

Chapter 44

DOWNSIZING REQUIRES QUALITY COMMUNICATION

No matter what the organizational, financial, or structural reasons for a merger, one thing that we must remember is that mergers, restructuring, downsizing, or "rightsizing" impact the lives of real people. And since people are at the heart of any organization, it is incumbent upon upper management to understand these human dynamics and how organizational change impacts on productivity and morale.

Abraham Maslow was right about his "hierarchy of needs." People can't focus on an organization's mission if they aren't confident that their basic needs will be taken care of. How can you get people to be enthusiastic about the big picture or to "get on board" with pending change, if they aren't sure that they can put food on their tables, pay the mortgage, or send their children to college?

Organizations, no matter how big or small, that ignore this reality do so at their own peril. You can't fudge this stuff. You can't fake it. People aren't stupid. They may not be looking forward to bad news, but they know on some level that straight talk from organizational leaders about difficult changes is better than the rumor mill.

When it comes to a merger or any major organizational restructuring, the truth—as it is known at a particular point in time—is the only reasonable communication strategy.

Is the truth painful? Often. But the alternative is far worse. The Harvard Business School has a truckload of case studies profiling organizations that have mishandled this communication challenge. Organizations often say they want to "maintain open lines of communication." Easier said than done.

Recently my friend Laura, who has been a staff attorney at Lucent Technologies for the past several years, agreed to a "voluntary" separation from the company. Hundreds of Laura's coworkers were laid off in a series of downsizings and restructurings. She said that ever since the downsizing started at Lucent, things have been uncertain at best and often tremendously frustrating. "Today, whether it's a voluntary separation, layoff or a reduction in work force, there are difficult issues that both employees and managers face in terms of keeping up morale, productivity and a semblance of sanity."

I asked Laura what, from her experience, are some of the biggest challenges facing managers in organizations where downsizing is a fact of organizational life. Further, what do most employees want from their manager?

"Regardless of the reason for the layoffs," she said, "each individual employee needs to feel that he or she is part of a cohesive unit. If you are one of the team players who are going to stay, you are aware that your workload is going to increase. You know that you are not going to have enough time to do your job and another person's job at the quality level the manager expects. Therefore, you need reassurance from the leader that you are all in this together."

In order to achieve this lofty goal, consider these tools for managing the internal communication process during times of major organizational change.

1. Provide timely, accurate, candid, and consistent information through a variety of vehicles including weekly newsletters, e-mail, focus groups, employee transition teams, staff meetings, and telephone hot-lines. The more people know about and understand the changes ahead, the less likely they are to start rumors and suffer from anxiety and reduced job effectiveness. Also, consider bringing in an outside consultant to facilitate a no-holds-barred dialogue between management and employees.

2. Never lie. Telling people that their jobs are secure when they're not only reduces an organization's credibility and creates further stress and distrust. Once trust is lost, the game is just about over.

3. Look to "surviving" employees in a merger or restructuring to design ways to make the adjustments easier. Listen to their suggestions and ask them what they need to get through this change. Allow them to come together and create some of the solutions. Don't just communicate from the top down. "Two-way" communication is a smart investment in the future of your redesigned organization.

4. Don't try to stifle or suppress employee venting and/or frustration over certain aspects of the merger. Some people need to express their anger in order for them to ultimately come to accept what is happening. Remember, for good reason, this is a grieving process for many employees. Put yourself in their position. How would you feel?

5. It is essential to provide counseling and training to employees—those who survive as well as those who are laid off. It is not only the humane thing to do, it's smart business. It builds goodwill. It lets people know you give a damn about them as people who have helped build an organization that, for whatever reason, is about to undergo a major change.

Managers must empathize with their workers who stay as well as those who go. They must communicate with candor and compassion. Further, they can't let their own fear of an uncertain future stop them from leading.

Chapter 45

CHANGE CAN BE GOOD

People often say that change is good. Change, they say, keeps us on our toes and ready to turn obstacles into opportunities. These people are sure that change is not only something important in our personal lives, but also crucial to the health of organizations. Well, if change is so good, then why is it so darn hard? And why do so many change efforts in business fail miserably? Here are some of the biggest reasons:

Organizational leaders don't understand how hard change is. Too many become highly impatient with employees who slow down the process—and let them know it. That only makes the change harder to implement.

Let's think about this. How leaders see change is one thing. They are the ones often driving the process. However, employees see it differently. They are the ones that the change is happening to. Successful change agents understand that they must empathize and understand the position of their employees and communicate accordingly. It's not clear that the change actually has to take place. The problem here is that many people in the organization don't believe the change is necessary. The key is for those leading change to communicate that the status quo is actually more dangerous and risky than the change. Until that's done, people have little or no motivation to "buy in" to the process. People are naturally resistant to change and therefore changing is unnatural. This fact of life cannot be ignored.

There's no opportunity to discuss the change in an open forum. People need to have the chance to express their concerns, issues, or questions about the change. If management doesn't allow for that, people will become frustrated and resist the change even more. They may say they are on board, but their actions will show that they are not. Smart managers create an environment that is conducive to an honest dialogue. Bad managers try to force-feed the change and then delude themselves into thinking people are on board when they are not. Open dialogue can be created in forums, employee meetings, interactive e-mails, and employee newsletters.

It's unclear what the change will produce. Change for the sake of change has little value. Too many people push for a change but do a poor job of explaining where the change will take the organization. What is the vision? How does the change connect to the bigger picture?

Too many organizations try to sell the change through detailed, standard-operating-procedure manuals or highly detailed descriptions of the steps needed to implement the change. This won't work if people aren't convinced that the end result of the change will be a good thing.

Management chooses to ignore obstacles that get in the way of change. According to John Kotter, an expert on change management who has examined over 100 companies trying to re-engineer themselves, "Sometimes the obstacle is organizational structure. . . . Sometimes compensation or performance appraisal systems make people choose between the new vision and their own self-interest. . . . Worst of all are the bosses who refuse to change and who make demands that are inconsistent with the overall effort." Whatever the obstacles to change are, they must be addressed and overcome. If there are particular people in the organization who are resisting change, those people must be convinced that it is in their interest to be a part of the transformation. To ignore obstacles is to invite failure.

Chapter 46

SWIMMING WITH THE FISHES

"There is always a choice about the way you do your work, even if there is not a choice about the work itself." This quote is taken from a great little book called *Fish: A Remarkable Way to Boost Morale and Improve Results,* written by Stephen Lundin. *Fish* is the story of the Pike Place Fish Market in Seattle, a workplace filled with energy, excitement, and enthusiasm. It's also the story of a fictitious company called First Guarantee and their Operations Group, which is characterized as "unresponsive, unpleasant, negative and zombie-like."

Mary Jane Ramirez, a smart, talented manager at the company, is assigned to take over the Operations Group and she's not happy about it. Like so many others in the company, Mary Jane is convinced that little, if anything, can be done to turn this team around. She thinks that much of the problem is in the mundane nature of the work itself. People are bored with the work and most of them have sent out their resumés, seeking other employment. The rest of the company refers to the group as a "toxic energy dump."

One day Mary Jane takes a walk to the Pike Place Fish Market.

Immediately she sees a fish flying through the air and she hears one of the workers yell out, "One salmon, flying away to Minnesota." The guy on the other end makes an unbelievable one-handed catch and takes a bow as the crowd watching the action applauds. As he continues to catch fish he engages in a playful dialogue with several people in the crowd. Mary Jane can't believe her eyes. People are laughing, working hard, and selling an awful lot of fish.

She then meets Lonnie, a manager at the fish market. Mary Jane tells Lonnie how impressed she is with the way the market is run. She asks Lonnie what the secret is in getting people to feel so good about what they do. Lonnie assures her that "it's not just about throwing fish."

Lonnie goes on to talk about the four keys to creating an energy-filled and exciting workplace. First . . . Choose the attitude you bring to work each day, even if the work itself isn't particularly exciting. The one thing you can control in life is your attitude. I know of a lot of people with great jobs, who make a ton of money, but have a terrible attitude.

Lonnie's second rule is to make sure you "play." He insists that any workplace, no matter how serious the work, must be a place where people can kid each other as well as the customers in an easy, comfortable fashion. But he tells Mary Jane not to misunderstand, and reminds her that you need to be serious about your business and the bottom line, but it's also ok to have a little fun while you're at it.

Next secret . . . Make the customer's day. Lonnie, the fish guy, says customers like to be part of the show. They want to be engaged and welcomed in on the fun. Clearly, for the fish market, this creates a lot of repeat business. The key is to break down barriers between the employee and the customer and to create a sense that you're all in this together. Finally, Lonnie explains how important it is to be "present." He talks about the significance of really listening, not just to customers, but to coworkers without doing ten other things that distract you. Don't you hate it when you are at a store counter and the clerk is either on the phone or on the computer? They just aren't present.

Mary Jane is moved by what she sees and hears at the fish market. Though skeptical, she attempts to implement some of their principles at her workplace.

First Mary Jane brings her team members to the fish market to witness for themselves what it is like to work in a positive, fun-filled, yet productive environment. Mary Jane's colleagues are greatly impressed, but aren't convinced that these principles will work on their team.

Then, Mary Jane separates her staff into four teams based on the four keys to success espoused by Lonnie. She gives the teams six weeks to meet, collect information, and put together a presentation to be given to the entire group. Each presentation must have action items that are doable. The results of her experiment are revealing. Even the most cynical team members find themselves caught up in the project.

The group focusing on incorporating more "play" into the Operations Group comes up with a series of action items: (1) Post signs saying, "THIS IS A PLAYGROUND. WATCH OUT FOR ADULT CHILDREN"; (2) add more life with plants and an aquarium; (3) start a joke-of-the-month contest; (4) arrange lunchtime events like having a live comedian.

The team working on "making the customer's day" offers these suggestions: (1) stagger work hours so there is coverage from 7:00 A.M. to 6:00 P.M., which will not only be helpful to customers, but also to employees with different needs; (2) organize focus groups of customers and ask them what they want and need from the Operations Group; (3) establish a monthly and annual award for service based on the recommendations of customers whose "day was made" by someone on the Operations team.

The "be fully present" team decides to make themselves role models for great listening when dealing with coworkers and customers. They support one another when a team member seems less than present, by establishing the code phrase "you seem distracted," as a signal for the person to work harder to be present. They also agree never to answer e-mails while talking on the phone with a colleague or customer. What a great idea. Every time I do try to multitask in this way (thinking it's more efficient communication), I wind up missing an important piece of information or misunderstanding someone's intent.

Finally, the "choose your attitude" team prepares an attitude "menu" for everyone in the Operations Group. The menu has two sides—one side is a frowning face attached to the words "angry," "bitter," and "uninterested." On the other side of the menu is a smiling face with the words "energetic," "caring," "supportive," and "creative" included. Across the top of the menu is the following title in bold print; "THE CHOICE IS YOURS."

While positive change didn't happen overnight, within a year the Operations Group had a whole new energy to it. They were also much more productive. No, the work wasn't necessarily more interesting, but the employees' approach to it was dramatically different.

In the end, attitude is everything, isn't it?

Chapter 47

NASA: A PROBLEM OF CULTURE

Much of what happens in professional life is the product of "culture"—organizational culture, to be more specific. These are the unwritten mores and values of an organization. You won't find any of these rules in writing. You won't find them in an organizational chart or the standard-operating-procedures manual. Yet, organizational culture is very real. It drives not only our successes, but our failures as well.

Consider the case of NASA, an organization I have conducted leadership training for. NASA is well respected and has accomplished great things over the years. However, NASA clearly has problems with its "culture." These were the findings of a much-awaited investigative report into the causes behind the recent *Columbia* disaster. Beyond the technical, mechanical, and space-related problems with the *Columbia*, much of the tragedy centered on NASA's culture, which had gone unexamined for too long. These are some of the same cultural issues that were raised after the *Challenger* disaster in 1986, but largely ignored.

- In many ways, the NASA culture discouraged scientists, managers, and others in the organization who were concerned about safety issues from communicating those concerns in public. According to the final report on the *Columbia* accident, meetings at NASA were tightly controlled by those in charge and information largely flowed in one direction—downward from the top. The report also found that numerous employees at NASA had written e-mails expressing safety concerns but never sent them. When interviewed, these NASA employees said they were afraid of being ridiculed.

- According to Senator Bill Nelson, a Florida Democrat, the *Columbia* accident was a product of a "lack of communication" and an "atmosphere of arrogance." This wasn't only Senator Nelson's opinion. The report produced from the *Columbia* investigation found that many top-level managers at NASA were so concerned about the organization's public reputation that they created an atmosphere in which any negative feedback was stifled for fear of hurting the organization's image.

- The NASA culture also apparently defined loyalty as going along with the status quo. This is ironic because under different leadership a healthier view of loyalty to NASA might have encouraged employees to raise concerns because of a deep commitment to the organization and a desire to see it be the best it could be.

- It also seems the NASA organizational culture has been quite insular. Concerns expressed by those outside the organization were often ignored. There may have been a sense within the organization that only those at NASA could understand the challenges and pressures facing this highly publicized federal agency.

My objective is not to pile criticism on NASA at this crucial point in its history. NASA's culture problems are not unique to them. These are problems inherent in countless public- and private-sector entities. However, NASA's particular problems present a unique opportunity for us to understand how organizational culture, even in an organization with top-notch professionals, can go awry. The message here is for all leaders, managers, and others to pay attention to the culture and not take it for granted. Certainly, there is no perfect organizational culture and no one-size prototype that fits all. However, when an organization discourages open, candid, and free-flowing information and communication, bad things are bound to happen. From every indication, that was a lot of the problem at NASA.

Chapter 48

FBI AND CIA:
NOT ON THE SAME PAGE

After September 11, 2001, you would have thought that the federal agencies involved in antiterrorism efforts would have joined together and started communicating like they were on the same team. But old habits die hard, and whether it's the federal government trying to bring agencies together or a corporation trying to get competing departments to stop feuding, achieving honest communication is hard. Some of the barriers to real communication within and between organizations involve such things as bad history, unhealthy competition, fear, distrust, and just plain laziness.

While there's a lot of talk about antiterrorism, there is also a long tradition of organizations like the FBI, CIA, FAA, and INS hoarding information and building barriers. They communicate with each other, but often not by choice and not in a timely and collegial fashion. The creation of a new super-organization in no way guarantees that the players involved in antiterrorism efforts will all of a sudden stop protecting their turf and start communicating. This is not a commentary about terrorism or even the federal government, but rather, it's about how insulated we can all become in our own organizations, and how this affects our communication with others.

When you're really on the same team, you're not afraid to share crucial information and communicate openly. The FBI had lots of valuable information in its field offices in Phoenix, Minneapolis, and Oklahoma regarding possible warning signs before September 11. However, that information never found its way into the hands of key decision makers at the Bureau. Further, that information wasn't shared with the CIA and other federal agencies dealing with terrorism. The fact is, even when there is a clear goal like fighting terrorism, it doesn't guarantee that those involved will communicate. According to a congressional investigator, there is a "longstanding historical problem" at the FBI in which "special agents in charge of field offices are like princes with their own little princedoms and the director is like the king who doesn't necessarily have the power to rein them in."

Whether you're a king, a CEO, the head of the FBI, or the president, you can't force people to communicate and act as if they're really on the same team. Productive, honest communication comes only when the individuals involved believe that their collective destiny is tied to other team members. That's not what's happening in Washington now. Those involved in the antiterrorism effort aren't convinced that they really need each other. They are not convinced that they will be rewarded for sharing and penalized if they don't. Until they are convinced, they will continue to protect their turf as well as their hides. They will share information only when forced to and communication will continue to be guarded and less than candid. No super-agency, no matter how big, is going to change that. None of this can be good, especially when the stakes are so high for all of us.

Chapter 49

PLANS FOR MY SUCCESSION: ARE YOU NUTS?

In 2004, top executives at CBS wanted to dump eighty-year-old Don Hewitt, the creator and executive producer of *60 Minutes*. CBS brass wanted to replace Hewitt with a forty-seven-year-old producer they thought was better for the job. Don Hewitt said, "No way." He said that he was at the top of his game and that he would "die at his desk. Hopefully at CBS." Eventually, top brass agreed to keep him on for a while and ease in the newcomer. However, it was clear that CBS and Hewitt hadn't done a particularly good job in executive succession planning. And a lack of succession planning for on-air talent was also manifested with the retirement of Dan Rather. They are not the only ones with this problem. Countless organizations, academic institutions, and nonprofit organizations don't do succession planning very well, either.

Although creating succession plans is an essential part of executive leadership, it is a very difficult task. It forces people to deal not only with management and leadership issues but also with an executive's own mortality and dispensability. The idea that an executive could get killed in a plane crash or car accident is terrifying. But, the fact is, these things happen. And there are other reasons for executive shuffling. Talented execs are offered other opportunities. They move on, and they move up. As with Don Hewitt, executives get older, and sometimes in spite of how they see themselves, they are just not as effective as they used to be.

But no matter how old or young, the really great executives make serious plans for replacing themselves. One executive who takes succession planning seriously is Annette Catino, CEO of QualCare. Catino recently held a retreat with her senior management team to deal with this issue. Her approach was unique. She told her staff to consider the following scenario: It was Monday morning and Annette hadn't been heard from. Soon, word was sent that she had been in an accident and had been hospitalized in serious condition. It was not clear when or if she was coming back. She then told her staff to figure out what should happen next and who would be in charge. Then, she walked out of the room for the next several hours. At first, her senior team was stunned, but after a while, they started putting the pieces together.

This is just one approach to getting your people to take seriously the prospect that you won't be there forever. But regardless of the approach, this thorny issue must be dealt with. However, certain conditions must be in place before implementing a succession plan:

1. The executive in question has to be psychologically and emotionally ready. Check your ego at the door. You are not indispensable regardless of how talented, charismatic, and effective you may be as a leader. Further, you shouldn't try to make yourself indispensable; you should help your organization plan for what happens if you are not there.

2. The senior management team must have enough depth and talent as well as maturity to deal with these questions and issues. They must have a history of working as a team and respecting each other.

3. The CEO's preference for who should be "in charge" must be made clear before the senior management team attempts to do any succession planning. If this preference is not clear and tacitly agreed to by the organization's board of directors as

well as the management team, it is an invitation for power struggles.

4. Executives must seek opportunities to have the organization run without them. Vacations and other instances where the executive is "out of the office" should be seen as an opportunity to determine how the senior management team functions, especially with the "temporary" leader in charge.

Chapter 50

YANKEES' MANAGER TORRE: A GREAT LEADER ON ANY FIELD

I'm a life-long Yankees fan. I have three sons who are forced to root for the Yankees. I actually believed in the curse of the Bambino for many years. That's why it was so hard for me when the "curse" was shattered by the Boston Red Sox in the 2004 American League Championship Series. Who knew that the Red Sox would come back to beat the Yankees after being down three games to one? It had never happened before. This chapter is a case study of Yankees manager Joe Torre that was written before the sad (for me) event of October 2004. Even though the Yankees aren't world champions this year, there is still a lot we can all learn from Joe Torre.

Hundreds of books have been written about different styles and models of leadership—clearly, there is no one way to lead or to communicate with your team. This is probably why I have always been fascinated by how leaders, managers, and coaches connect with their people. After watching and exploring the leadership styles of thousands of people, the one team leader who stands out above the crowd is Yankees manager Joe Torre.

For those of you saying "baseball isn't like business," forget it. People are people. Even ballplayers making millions of dollars to play a little kid's game sulk, argue, and get down on themselves. Just as employees in the workplace need to be motivated to get over a slump, so do Cy Young Award-winning pitchers like Roger Clemens and superstar shortstops like Derek Jeter.

Joe Torre is such a success as Yankees manager largely because of his extraordinary skills as a communicator. He knows when to push, prod, leave alone, or just listen. He's not one of these rah-rah "win it for the Gipper" leaders. Rather, he treats his players like the professionals that they are. Most importantly, he treats them like individuals who have their own peculiar or unique set of personal characteristics, quirks, and idiosyncrasies.

In his book *Ground Rules for Winners,* Torre dedicates an entire chapter to what he calls "Straight Communication: The Key to Trust." Torre says communication is the key to trust and trust is the key to teamwork in any group endeavor, be it sports, business, or family.

Consider these highlights of Joe Torre's successful strategy for communicating and connecting with his players: Know the needs of each player, whether it's support, motivation, reassurance, or technical help. The Yankees manager also says that a few words of appreciation or a simple "good job" and a pat on the back can go a long way to motivate and focus team players. This is an area that many managers ignore because they assume their players (or employees) know that the boss thinks they're doing a good job. Don't assume. If you think someone on your team is doing a good job, say so.

Lots of managers in the workplace have really bad timing when it comes to communicating with their people. We must determine when "the door is open" (for communication), says Torre. "If you don't find the right time to say it, all your good intentions will go up in smoke."

Ironically, while Torre has an excellent sense of timing in his communication with his players, Yankees owner George Steinbrenner is among the worst in this area. Steinbrenner believes that all players respond well at all times to public criticism and a kick in the butt. Conversely, it is Torre's patience that has allowed Steinbrenner to get the most out of his very diverse and highly paid team.

Finally, Torre says that it's critical to get issues out on the table and deal with problems in a candid fashion. But beyond candor, Torre believes that clarity and civility are the other qualities that are essential to "straight communication and building trust." He also adds that you can express anger effectively without resorting to screaming tantrums. The Yankees manager believes in leading with a velvet glove rather than an iron fist. George Steinbrenner and other "bosses" of his ilk could benefit greatly from Joe Torre's advice.

At Work

Chapter 51

JOB HUNTERS NEED TO PREPARE

Being downsized? Right-sized? Unexpectedly find yourself looking for a new job? Landing on your feet in the unpredictable employment world often comes down to how well you communicate. How well you communicate is largely played out in job interviews. Most professionals don't do well in interviews. They are overly nervous, unfocused, talk too much, and don't ask the right questions of a prospective employer. Sure, you have to be in the right, positive frame of mind ("I'm good. I can do this job!"). But, succeeding in an interview comes down to how well you prepare and then present yourself.

GET TO THE POINT . . . QUICKLY. Don't ramble. If you are going on for more than a minute straight, wind down fast. According to Robin Ryan, author of the book *Sixty Seconds and You're Hired,* "In today's fast paced world, we often focus on things for less than 60 seconds. . . . Nervousness and no preparation often result in long, continuous, never ending answers."

PRACTICE. Do a mock job interview for a job you think you want. Get into the habit of responding to questions and speaking in concise, compelling sound bites. The key is to be disciplined. But the only way to be disciplined is to do a dress rehearsal. Even the Yankees' Derek Jeter works out the kinks in spring training.

DEVELOP THREE KEY SELLING POINTS. Few people can re-member more than three main points, especially when they've interviewed dozens of people before you and there are another dozen waiting in the reception area.

DO A SERIOUS SELF-ASSESSMENT. Take a sheet of paper and draw a line down the middle. On the left side, list your greatest strengths as a professional. On the right side, list what you need to work on. Focus on your strengths, then prioritize them. Con-nect your top three selling points with the position you are seek-ing. Don't expect to walk in and have those selling points at your fingertips if you haven't done the work.

PROVE YOUR POINT. Make these three selling points come alive with compelling examples and anecdotes about your work history. If you are interviewing for a job as the head of fundrais-ing, say something like, "I'm an excellent and very creative fund-raiser." (Oh yeah? prove it!) "Over the past two years, I led our organization's fundraising and we brought in over $3 million through a variety of events, auctions, and a direct mail cam-paign that I designed." Prospective employees need specifics to make your claim of being good at this or that believable.

BE AN EXCEPTIONAL AND ACTIVE LISTENER. Don't inter-rupt when you are being asked a question. Make sure you know exactly what is being asked. Don't focus so much on your an-swers that you miss the nuance of what an employer is looking for. If you are not sure, being an active listener means that you should ask clarifying questions such as, "Do you have an example?"

CUSTOMIZE YOUR RESPONSE. Avoid generic answers. Mi-chelle Lubaczewski, assistant director of the Career Services Employment Center at Rutgers University–New Brunswick says that in an interview, the "cookie cutter" response will not work. Instead, customize your response to the needs of the organiza-tion. You must connect with employers and let them know that you know and respect them. Do your homework and research the company to know its goals, products, and other specific de-tails that you can use in your responses.

MAINTAIN YOUR MOMENTUM. Give yourself an "energy check" every few minutes to make sure you are projecting and enunciating your voice. Many times people will lose their focus, thereby losing the edge with a prospective employer.

TURN THE TABLES. They are not only interviewing you, you are interviewing them. Find out where the interviewer is in the company, how he or she got there, his or her view of the company and what direction he or she feels the company is going in to see if this company is a good fit for you. It is important to ask solid questions to determine whether you really want to work there. The key is to do this without being pushy, cocky, or arrogant while always maintaining respect for the employer and their organization.

Chapter 52

INVEST EARLY IN NEW EMPLOYEES

New people come into organizations all the time. Too often, critical communication mistakes are made and opportunities are missed early on. Bad habits are developed and unhealthy patterns are established. If you wait too long, it becomes extremely difficult to fix the situation, and those new employees become less than productive.

With this in mind consider the following tips to bring a new employee on board and establish a communication foundation that you can build upon:

- Standard-operating procedures and employee manuals are fine, but too often they are filled with useless information and reams of data that have little to do with the person's job and what is expected of him or her. Instead, develop a more streamlined written manual that has basic office policies, functions of equipment, important phone numbers, vacation policies, etc. Be as specific as possible and include a section entitled, "Questions Most Commonly Asked by Employees."

- Set aside some valuable face time in the first few days of the employee's tenure. If you hired the person directly, make sure you make yourself available. This doesn't have to be in the office. In fact, sometimes it is better to do it over a cup of coffee or lunch in a relaxed and informal setting. Your objective is to break down the barriers and establish an open line of communication where any question can be asked or any issue raised.

- Don't confuse such sit-downs with bull sessions. They are not. Therefore, you should go into them with a clear, written agenda. Informal and relaxed doesn't mean disorganized and haphazard. Such an agenda might include the following: mistakes to avoid; areas of work to prioritize; key people (internally and externally) to touch base with, etc.

- Establish a preferred method of communicating. Some organizations thrive on meetings to share valuable information and make key decisions. If that's the case, say so. Make it clear how important meetings are and how the new employee should prepare for them. However, in other organizations, e-mail and/or telephone communication drive the organization's success. If that's the case, establish e-mail and phone communication within the first few days.

- Style matters. For example, tell the employee you like brief, concise, bullet-point e-mails where key questions are raised and issues are put on the table. Further, communicate how decisions will be made. For example, don't tell a new employee to "be assertive." Rather, tell him or her to make a recommendation on a course of action and get your feedback by a certain date. If you don't respond that means you want the employee to move on it. This will avoid the type of communication bottlenecks that often hurt productivity.

- Have key people in the organization sit down with the new employee. Don't leave it to chance that valuable information will be shared around the water cooler. If you know a particular manager can be especially helpful to the new employee, schedule a sit-down and make it clear to both parties why you are doing it. The key is for the new hire to get the lay of the land from a variety of sources.

- If possible, assign a mentor or coach to the new hire. In the process, establish specific goals regarding individual performance. Monitor the coaching process without micromanaging it. Then, at key intervals, say three and six months, sit down with the new employee and his or her mentor to review progress and make recommendations for improvement.

Chapter 53

HANDLING EMPLOYEE COMPLAINTS

The workplace is filled with employees that are unhappy and have complaints. Sometimes, you are not sure where these complaints are coming from or what the employee's real motivation is. Yet, regardless of their origin, the feelings of team members matter a great deal. With this in mind, consider some tips and tools for managers dealing with employee gripes:

Have a genuine open-door policy. A lot of people talk about having it, but few actually do. Your employees/team members really need to know that they can approach you openly and honestly and tell you how they feel. If they are afraid to voice a complaint, their frustration will only fester and will ultimately impact on individual and organizational productivity. The easier it is to approach you, the more likely it is that your employees actually will.

Allow for anonymous complaints. Sometimes, people may have legitimate concerns, but they don't want to be identified as the person who expressed them. An organization needs to allow for people to maintain their confidentiality if the issue they raise is so sensitive that they feel no matter how open you or your door are, the risk is just too great.

Simplify standard-operating procedures. Many organizations have standard-operating procedures or rules for how to communicate complaints. Having an organized system makes sense, but sometimes there are so many barriers and obstacles that get in the way (in order to follow the rules) that employees say to themselves, "It is not worth the trouble." Make sure your organization is not using standard-operating procedures as a mechanism to stifle employee concerns and create unnecessary layers of bureaucracy.

Strive to empathize. One of the hardest things to do as a manager is to be patient with and open-minded to an employee complaint when you think it makes absolutely no sense. (I know, I've been in that situation.) But remember, as rational as you think you may be, you are only seeing the situation from your point of view. If you don't empathize and try to gain the employee's perspective, your frustration will show.

Take time to respond. Listening to an employee complaint doesn't mean you need to make an immediate decision about the situation. Resist the temptation to "solve the problem" right on the spot unless it is absolutely clear to you what the solution is. Try to be patient. Listen and then tell the employee you want to get some additional information and think about it.

Ask the employee for a solution. Very often employees are good at communicating what is bothering them, but have a hard time identifying a potential solution. Your job is to get them to think about how to turn the situation around. The conversation could go like this, "John, you have made it clear that you really don't like working with Jane. But given that the two of you are key members of our team, what would you like to see done?" In certain instances, John might say, "Get rid of Jane." Again, if this happens, practice patience and respond with a follow-up question. "Frankly, John, that's not a realistic option. So given that, what exactly would make things better for you so that you can be more productive?"

Finally, close the loop. Whatever is agreed upon, make sure it is communicated and a follow-up procedure is put in place. More specifically: "Great, John, so we have agreed that you and Jane would only work together on projects A, B, and C. Please send me a weekly update on how things are going with those projects. In three months, we will revisit the situation and decide where to go from there."

Chapter 54

DON'T HOLD A MEETING IF . . .

There are countless meetings held every day that don't have to be called and are seen by many as a tremendous waste of time. So instead of talking about how to hold more effective meetings, let's look at the meeting issue from a different perspective. Let's ask whether you should hold a meeting at all. With that in mind, don't hold a meeting if . . .

Don't hold a meeting if all you really want to do is hear yourself talk. We all know managers who hold meetings just to have an audience. Wanting to hear yourself talk is not a good enough reason to call a meeting, and those who don't know that pay a heavy price, with those around them not taking them seriously and zoning out when the meeting is called. This is particularly dangerous when the time comes for a leader to hold a meeting about something really important. He or she winds up being the kid who cried wolf.

Don't hold a meeting if you can accomplish your goal through a brief conference call or e-mail. Once you call a meeting, the bar has been raised because you are asking people to physically do what they need to do to get to the meeting: to invest time and energy. Take more time up-front and explore other avenues to accomplish your goal. More often than not you will find that the telephone and/or e-mail is the more appropriate communication medium.

Don't hold a meeting if all you are looking to do is "rubber stamp" a decision you have already made. If you have no intention of listening to others' points of view or communicating in an open, interactive fashion, then don't insult people by getting them together. Just have the guts to communicate the decision you've made and let them know it is not negotiable and you don't really want their opinion. There is nothing worse than having meeting leaders tell you they want your input when it is clear in the end all they are looking to do is ram something down your throat.

Don't hold a meeting if your real motive is to communicate a certain message to a particular team member that you'd rather not do one on one. Meetings should not use participants as a shield or to camouflage what a leader is really looking to accomplish. First, everyone will know what you are doing and won't appreciate it. Second, such an approach sends a chilling message to employees about how you deal with conflict and what they can expect when and if you have an issue or problem with them.

Don't hold a meeting if your agenda is not clear-cut. This is similar to the first reason identified not to call a meeting, but it goes a step further. This assumes your goal is greater than simply to hear yourself talk, but acknowledges that even with the best of intentions, some meeting leaders are simply not prepared to call a meeting. They haven't thought through a concrete list of items and issues to address and want to believe that an agenda will automatically appear once the meeting is called. The problem is, it doesn't work that way. That's why too many meetings are rambling, unfocused, and go on way too long.

Simply put, the vast majority of meetings in the world of work don't need to be called. The most effective leaders and managers respect people's time. If you take this approach, you will get a heck of a lot more out of your team and they will appreciate you for it.

Chapter 55

LET'S MAKE A DEAL

Whether it is at work or at home, all of us are involved in negotiating nearly every day. We negotiate with our bosses and our kids, our coworkers and our spouses. But when you break down the art of negotiation, it's really about communication. It's about connecting and ultimately the art of compromise. As Herb Cohen, author of the classic book *You Can Negotiate Anything* and a new tome called *Negotiate This!*, says, "Negotiating is the game of life." It really is, when you think about it.

As someone who has had to negotiate contracts, fees, and sponsorship for PBS television programs, I've come to the following conclusions as to what it takes to be a first-rate negotiator:

- Great negotiators are great listeners. If you notice, they don't do a lot of talking but instead spend much of the time asking smart questions and concentrating on the answers. They also take their time responding to what they've heard as opposed to reacting in an unnecessarily adversarial fashion.

- Remember, even if you don't like the other person or his communication style, you're negotiating because you have to. If you could simply get your way, you wouldn't be in this situation. Therefore, no matter how you feel about the other party, stay focused on the issues that need to be resolved. The key is to remember that communicating your distaste decreases the odds you will accomplish your objectives. Simply put, focus more on the problem and less on the person.

- Communicate from the other person's point of view. Great negotiators work hard to see the process as an opportunity to help someone else accomplish his or her objective. When participants are too focused on their own (often narrow) objective, they aren't successful. If other people see you as someone who is considerate of them and their agenda, they are more likely to give you what you want without seeing it as giving in.

- Be clear on what you want, but don't dig your heels in too deep. It's important to communicate your goals in the negotiation process while being flexible enough to respond to opportunities that present themselves in the process. (Again, it is important to be a good listener.)
- If you go into a negotiation with a hard-and-fast definition of "winning," you are likely to be disappointed. And unless you are willing to walk away, this is a risky position to take indeed.
- When someone says something in a negotiation that seems totally unreasonable to you, don't take the bait. Very often the person is doing this to see what your reaction will be. I've seen many negotiations go awry at this critical point. Instead, remain calm. Imagine you are a manager who has an employee who is requesting a 30 percent pay increase. Consider this disarming response: "I just want to be clear, you are saying you want a 30 percent pay increase while we've just laid off a third of our workforce and everyone else's salary is frozen?" Your goal is to put a mirror in front of the other person and help him or her see how unreasonable that demand is. If the person doesn't, I would suggest this isn't someone you want to deal with. But that's a whole other issue.
- Finally, avoid characterizing someone's position as worthless ("That's a really stupid point, Jim"). When you communicate in this fashion, Jim feels worthless as a person and has few options other than to fight back and dig in. Is that what you really want?

Chapter 56

COMMUNICATION IS THE KEY TO GREAT TEAMWORK

Most of what goes on in the workplace takes place in teams. Lots of really smart or talented people don't succeed in the workplace because they are either unable or unwilling to work in teams. Usually, these people have weak interpersonal communication skills. Unless you are some sort of computer whiz, natural-born artist, or Tiger Woods, your success is too complex for you to succeed alone. Just like in kindergarten, we must be able to work and play well with others.

First, you can't be an effective team player if you aren't a good communicator. I don't mean simply being a "good talker." Some good talkers are the worst team players. Often, that's because they're terrible listeners. Team members need to listen to each other in order to succeed. Plus, I still believe in the old saying, "actions speak louder than words!"

Some of the characteristics of a really great team include: being clear on exactly what the team's goal is; team members knowing their role and how that role relates to the overall success of the team; team members having the tools necessary to fulfill their roles on the team; an open, supportive, collegial environment that encourages candid day-to-day dialogue regarding the team's challenges, opportunities, and obstacles; and team members being willing to take risks and propose new ideas without fear of reprisal.

There are some other characteristics great teams have, like trusting each other and taking each other and each others' comments at face value; an all-for-one-and-one for-all mentality in which team members jump in to help each other in a time of need. The key is to do this without keeping score of who's doing what for whom. The most productive and healthy teams have members who talk to each other in a civil and respectful manner. Feedback is encouraged and welcomed, and is always done in a constructive, positive fashion.

One more characteristic that great teams have is that any team member can step up and become a situational leader at any given time. Flexibility in the team structure and dynamic is critical for success.

When you think about it, none of this can be achieved without excellent communication among team members. The bottom line is that every great team needs one primary leader setting the tone and fostering an environment for team members to reach their individual potential and for the team overall to succeed. It's not by accident that the greatest leaders are often excellent communicators. Again, that doesn't just mean being a great talker.

Chapter 57

WORKPLACE DEBATING 101

Debating skills are critical to any professional who seeks to persuade workplace colleagues on important projects or initiatives. With this in mind, consider some tools that will help you in meetings, boardrooms, or any professional situation where debating skills are needed.

- Plan but don't cram. Of course you must know your subject matter, but too often people cram so much data into their head that by the time they are asked to argue their point of view, they are on information overload.
- Unlike high school or college forensics, debates aren't really about how much you know on a given topic. Instead, they are about how much conviction you have about the two or three main points you are communicating. If your audience believes you believe, you have a big debating edge.
- Have a plan but be flexible. Communicating key messages is critical, but sometimes in these public exchanges, opportunities arise that great communicators must seize. Being disciplined is not the same as being inflexible. So keep your eyes and your mind open.
- Your tone of voice matters. Be strong and confident when debating a colleague, but there is no reason to yell. Raising your

voice can communicate the message to others that you're actually not too sure of your position.

- When your workplace debate "opponent" is speaking, show respect. Look at him or her. Don't go through your notes or prepare for the next thing you want to say. Avoid sarcastic facial expressions. No rolling of the eyes.

- Speaking of nonverbal communication, stand, don't sit, if at all possible. Further, your posture matters. No slouching or swaying back and forth. Avoid leaning on a podium or conference table. Stand tall and erect, but don't be a wooden soldier.

- Of course you are there to argue a specific position; however, great workplace debaters aren't afraid to acknowledge a good point an opponent makes. Just don't do it too much or your audience will wonder how passionate you are about your position.

- Avoid canned one-liners. They are overrated and it is extremely difficult to deliver them at the right time without it seeming that you are forcing the issue.

- Disagree, but don't be disagreeable. Always be respectful of your debate opponent. No name-calling or dismissing his or her position with comments such as, "That's the dumbest argument I've ever heard, Bob!" Even if people agree with your content, they will be turned off by your style.

- Don't be afraid to smile. Even though it is a debate, one of the biggest problems debaters have is that they appear to take themselves and their position too seriously. You can be a professional and argue with conviction and still be relaxed and comfortable with yourself and the situation you are in.

- Identify three or four predictable points your opponent is likely to make and prepare to challenge him or her and shift the conversation back to your main message.

- When debating, avoid beginning sentences with qualifiers such as "I think" or "I believe." These phrases only weaken your argument and make you seem unsure.

- Finally, never interrupt a questioner, who is a potential decision maker, regarding the idea you are proposing. Let the full question be put on the table, then take a beat before responding. In debates and in most workplace situations, nobody likes a know-it-all.

Chapter 58

THE DANGERS OF MULTITASKING

Recently, two parents took their eleven-year-old son to the hospital for a stress test on his heart. As the doctor was reading the test results his beeper went off. He immediately asked the nurse/technician in charge to call his office. The doctor then proceeded to have a conversation with his office involving another patient case while reading the EKG results. At several points, while the doctor was talking with his office staff, the nurse running the EKG equipment thought the doctor was talking to her, and vice versa. This confusing, not to mention annoying, communication went on for several minutes until the doctor was confronted by one of the parents. Ultimately, the doctor apologized but explained that he was "very busy" and continued that he often felt the need to "multitask" because his plate was so full.

Doctors aren't alone. All of us multitask, but rarely do we think about the consequences of our actions or the impact multitasking has on the quality of our communication and the quality of our relationships with others. In the previous example, it is clear that the doctor was more prone to engage in miscommunication involving either or both medical cases because of his multitasking. His level of concentration was not what it needed to be. He was simply not present and that can be dangerous.

Consider some ways we multitask and the impact it has on our everyday communication:

- Conversing on the phone while checking e-mail or surfing the web. How many of us are guilty of this? While you think you are being productive, you run the risk of missing valuable pieces of information. Further, the nuance or subtleties of interpersonal communication often get lost unless you are truly concentrating on this single task. Simple advice: keep your computer screen off while talking on the phone, because the temptation to use it is too great.

- Working your Palm Pilot or reviewing reading material while participating in a meeting. Meetings can be boring and you may be justified by multitasking in this way. But again, important opportunities to contribute to the meeting's goals and to communicate your views will be missed while your attention is diverted.

- Going through a mental "to do" list while in a face-to-face conversation with a professional colleague or family member. Make a decision to be present. Commit to the conversation and raise the bar for your interpersonal communication. Fight the urge to go on "automatic pilot" and fake it. In most cases, the person you are speaking with will see that you are not present and become frustrated, or even worse, will mentally shut down.

- Engaging in a work-related conference call on a cell phone while driving in heavy traffic. (I've been guilty of this one!) Even if you are using your speakerphone or hands-free device, it is really risky to digitally dial a number on your cell phone when driving. Therefore, if you have to communicate via cell phone, pull off to the side of the road, particularly if the call's content is important. You will find that your communication is much better when you do this.

- Watching TV or listening to the radio (with all those annoying commercials) while going over important work-related material or, if a student, while doing homework or reading course material. Concentration is the key to more effective communication, both verbal and written.

Chapter 59

THOSE CONSTANT INTERRUPTIONS

All of us deal with interruptions in the workplace. It could be the phone ringing, "instant e-mails" that are crying out for an immediate response, colleagues walking into your office with something "really pressing," whether a work-related item or a crisis at home. Sometimes it's people coming in just to chat about what they did over the weekend.

Here's the problem: You go into work with a well-thought-out game plan as to what you want to accomplish that day. You have a to-do list, it's prioritized, and you are feeling really good about the next eight hours. All of a sudden, your plan begins to crumble because of the incessant interruptions. What do you do about it? You don't want to be rude and you want to be an accessible team player. You've always promoted this open door (or-cubicle) policy, but it's just not working anymore.

With this challenging workplace scenario in mind, consider some communication tips and tools to deal with interruptions:

- First, accept the fact that your action plan for the day is not set in stone. It's simply a guide to help you stay focused. Anticipate that there will be interruptions and that the plan will have to be modified. Don't let it throw you off. Take it in stride and take a deep breath. Don't be obsessed about accomplishing 100 percent of your to-do list. Figure out what absolutely has to be done today versus what can wait. Doing this will put you in a healthier frame of mind when the interruptions come and will improve the way you communicate with those around you.
- Redefine what it means to be "rude." Placating people by not being up front and honest about how their interruption is impacting your productivity is not doing anyone any favors. It's unfair to you, it communicates a false message to your colleague, and it cheats your organization. As a leader, help build a communication culture that promotes candor and directness with tact. So the next time Jane comes into your office just to chat while you are up against a deadline, say something like, "Jane, I'd love to chat, but I really have to get this Jones memo

out by 10:00 A.M. Can we catch up later over a cup of coffee?" Your objective is to communicate to Jane that while work comes first, being social is still important. It's all about balance.

- Consider what happens if you aren't up-front with Jane. She's telling you about her weekend while you're half listening and getting angry with her for keeping you from getting the Jones memo done on time. You're saying things like "uh-ha" and doing the occasional obligatory head nodding, but there is no connection. What's worse is the Jones memo will suffer and later on you'll blame Jane and be angry at yourself for not handling the situation more effectively.
- Let's talk telephones. You are in the middle of composing the Jones report while the phone keeps ringing. Why not try putting your phone on "do not disturb." The other option is to more effectively use Caller ID. Unless it is absolutely critical that you take that call right then, don't take the call. Just get the message and call back when you are in a clearer frame of mind.
- And what about electronic interruptions? E-mails constantly pouring into your mailbox. Rarely is it a matter that needs to be addressed immediately. Therefore, once again prioritize what needs to be done and don't get caught up in the desire to always have an empty electronic in-box. As we all know, the messages will still be there tomorrow.

Chapter 60

SPEAK SLOWLY, CLEARLY WHEN LEAVING A MESSAGE

A couple weeks ago, I got a telephone message from a producer at a radio station requesting an interview regarding a column I had written. The problem was, as I listened to the recording, I couldn't make out the name of the producer. I must have played the tape ten times. The only thing I could make out was that her name sounded like "three-fifty." In fact, I had a colleague listen to the tape and she said it sounded like "three-fifty." I don't want to embarrass the producer by actually publishing her name, but I assure you it wasn't "three-fifty."

My point is, it is amazing how many people don't know how to communicate effectively over the telephone. They either talk too fast, gargle their words, or speak so softly that you can't even hear them. Another ineffective circumstance is when someone calls me for business or, worse yet, a personal call, on speakerphone. Why can't they talk to me through the receiver? These are just some of the communication faux pas people make over the telephone.

Consider the following tips next time you are on the phone for business or pleasure:

1. It is always a good idea to ask people if it is okay for you to speak to them on speakerphone. Next, tell them who else is in the room. Also, when trying to negotiate or finalize an important business deal, never, and I mean *never*, do it over the speakerphone. It sends the wrong message.

2. When it comes to leaving voice messages, speak in a clear fashion. Slow down your rate of speech and actually think about what you want to say before you say it. In addition, keep your phone messages short and to the point.

3. It is also important to use simple, easy to understand English when leaving a message. Don't introduce any technical or complicated names of programs or services that will be unfamiliar to the receiver.

4. Another tool that helps me is to jot down a few bullet points on a Post-it Note before I place a business call. This serves as an outline and a reminder during a phone conversation as to the purpose of my call.

5. When in a phone conversation, be an attentive and active listener. Just as in face-to-face conversation, no one likes to be interrupted while they are talking.

6. Great listening isn't solely about being silent. Great telephone communicators ask good, open-ended follow-ups such as "tell me more" or "do you have an example of that?"

7. When you place your business calls is also critical. The best times I found are between 9 and 11:30 A.M. and between 2:30 and 5 P.M.

8. What about playing telephone tag? When e-mail is not an option and I'm trading calls with someone I really want to talk to, I leave a message listing several times that I will be available for a phone conversation. I then ask the other party to confirm one of those times. My limit is three messages for someone before I stop calling. Any more than that you look desperate.

Another good telephone tip: If you do want to do business with someone, return calls within twenty-four hours.

Chapter 61

USING POWERPOINT?
BETTER HAVE A PLAN B

Todd Edelson is a physical therapist and educator who has been making presentations for over fifteen years. He is also a dedicated student of communication who is fascinated by presentation tools and techniques that work, as well as those that fall short. Edelson is a big believer in low-tech communication that is simple and to the point.

Recently, Edelson was scheduled to give a major presentation at a local university on the biomechanics of a disc. The dean in charge met Edelson before the presentation and asked what PowerPoint he intended to use. Edelson informed him that he had no PowerPoint presentation. "What about the university helping you to develop some slides or overheads?" Edelson responded that all he needed were blank overheads that he could fill in during the presentation. "Just then I saw a bead of sweat coming down this guy's forehead," said Edelson. "I'm sure he thought, 'This guy is totally unprepared. We made a big mistake bringing him in.'"

Then Edelson showed the dean his "bag of toys" and informed him that it was all he needed for the presentation. He also invited the nervous administrator into the seminar, saying that if he didn't like what he saw after half an hour, they could try a different approach. Incidentally, the bag of toys Edelson brought in were a bunch of cheap children's toys known as a "boink" (the ninety-nine-cent finger trap you would find on the boardwalk). The boink was passed out to every seminar participant while Edelson explained how the mechanics of the boink mirrored the mechanics of the disc. It was simple, fun, and memorable. How's that for low-tech?

Many professionals have become enamored with high-tech bells and whistles, particularly PowerPoint. Some are convinced that the more high-tech, the better the presentation. Yet, low-tech communication isn't only acceptable, it is often preferable. Even if they have a PowerPoint presentation, the really good communicators are prepared to move to plan B if and when the technology breaks down, which it often does.

Todd Edelson tells of a time he attended a conference in Orlando, Florida, in which a nationally recognized expert on back pain was scheduled to give a presentation before 500 people. Right before the presentation began, Edelson turned to his associate and said, "I wonder what this guy would do if his PowerPoint didn't work?" Just then, the presenter's PowerPoint broke down.

After the first slide, everything went blank. According to Edelson, the presenter immediately panicked and started fumbling with the technology, while continuing to apologize. For the next fifteen to twenty minutes, he decided to tell everyone what he was doing to "fix it." Finally, the technology kicked in. By this point, the audience had checked out. Undaunted, the presenter sped through what was scheduled to be a thirty-minute PowerPoint presentation in less than five minutes and then concluded by saying, "Thank goodness I've had a lot of experience as an extemporaneous speaker." Edelson thought, "You've got to be kidding. I've learned nothing from this."

Some people are confused in thinking that the message is in the technology. It's not. The message is in you. What the presenter in Orlando should have done was tried once, maybe twice, to get the PowerPoint working and then made a humorous aside about it. Then, he could have stepped away from the technology, and talked directly to his audience. He should have had a simple, bulleted outline of key points. He should have had a low-tech version of his high-tech presentation. If he had a slide referring to a particular study, he should have had a corresponding plain piece of paper with that same information. But the presenter had none of this and missed an opportunity to stand, deliver, and connect with his audience in a powerful way.

The technology didn't break down. The presenter broke down and had no one else to blame but himself.

Chapter 62

POWERPOINT IS GREAT IF . . .

I am not a big fan of PowerPoint. Too many people hide behind it in too many situations where they should just be "talking" to people. Yet, I have seen PowerPoint used effectively on a few occasions. One of the best high-tech presenters I've worked with is Dr. Harold Paz.

Although Dr. Paz is an avid PowerPoint user, he is not obsessed with the bells and whistles of the technology. He uses it only when it enhances his presentation technique. In a recent presentation before a group of medical and healthcare professionals, Paz demonstrated some of the fine points of a PowerPoint presentation. Here were some of the highlights:

- Dr. Paz's presentation was only twenty minutes, which he cut down from the forty he originally planned. That's editing 50 percent of your content. It required cutting out a lot of slides that were near and dear to his heart, but were not appropriate given the busy conference agenda scheduled that day. The moral is, less is usually more.
- There was very little information on each slide. For example, on a bold blue background, Dr. Paz attempted to communicate specific information regarding the number of medical students at his school. He used three bullet-pointed statistics.

One was in red, one was in blue, and the other in yellow. Each number stood out and was easy to follow.

- On another individual slide where there was a significant amount of information, the doctor went through only certain points that were relevant for this particular audience in this specific setting. The key to remember is that you don't have to explain every piece of information on a slide.

- Keep things moving. Paz didn't stay on any one slide too long. He didn't get bogged down in the minutia of his presentation. Rather, he kept his pacing without making his audience feel rushed. This approach also communicates the message that the presentation isn't going to last forever, which is usually our greatest fear.

- The doctor also used a map to signify important pieces of information. This map had certain sections highlighted that helped him make his point about medical education. A map like this is much more effective than simply listing your information on a PowerPoint slide.

- A picture can be worth a thousand words. When trying to explain that the medical school incorporated "small group classrooms," there was a picture of a class with a small group of students and a teacher leading the discussion. This picture is a much more effective tool than simply having a slide that says, "our school has a small number of students in each class."

- Bar charts are a great tool. When attempting to show that the school has taken in an increasing amount of grant dollars, a bar chart from 1992 to 2002 dramatically demonstrated this fact. Again, it is much more effective to visually see the contrast as opposed to having a slide that simply says, "our school has taken in X more dollars in grants in the past ten years."

- Finally, Dr. Paz showed a cover of *US News and World Report* highlighting the work of his medical school. Again, this is a perfect example of what PowerPoint can be. Saying it is one thing. Seeing it is another.

Bottom line? While PowerPoint is often overused and misused, when it is done right, it can add a great deal to any presentation. It's just too bad that a presentation like Dr. Paz's seems to be the exception.

Chapter 63

TIPS FOR COMPANY PARTIES

Whether it's the winter holiday party or the summer company picnic, there are often times when we must mix business with pleasure. While these events can be great fun, they can also be filled with anxiety and potentially awkward situations. Here are a few tips to help you make the most of social gatherings with colleagues and clients.

1. Smile! It's a powerful way to send the message that you are a friendly and open person. It also puts you and the other person in a positive frame of mind to converse.

2. Be the first to say "hello." By being the one to break the ice, it allows you to gently guide the conversation.

3. Maintain relaxed, yet focused eye contact when in a conversation and avoid what I call "cocktail party eyes." This is that annoying habit of looking past the person you are talking with because someone "more interesting" walks by. Think of how you would feel if someone did that to you. It's downright rude.

4. Unless you know someone really well, avoid discussing heavy topics such as race relations, politics, or religion. Even though these topics can make for fascinating conversation, they can also get out of hand, especially when people are drinking.

5. Once the ice is broken, bring up casual topics such as kids ("So how old are your children now?"), houses ("Didn't you just move into a new home?"), work ("What line of work are you in?"), sports ("Wasn't that Subway Series amazing?"), the stock market ("This market is like a roller coaster."), hobbies ("We just went on a hiking trip and we had such a great time."), movies you've just seen ("We took the kids to see that Grinch movie. It wasn't bad."), or restaurants you've just been to ("We just moved into the area. Do you know of a good Italian restaurant close by?").

6. Get people to talk about themselves and avoid talking too much about yourself and all of the great and exciting things

going on in your life or business. Most people love to be asked questions about themselves, their work, or their families. ("That's a great dress you're wearing, Mary. If you don't mind me asking, where did you get it?")

7. Back to the alcohol issue. Holiday cocktail parties can create some weird communication situations. I was recently at a party where the wife of a prominent business executive got really smashed. She was slurring her words and spilling her drink all over the place. It was embarrassing for her, her husband, and the people who wound up in a conversation with her. Sure, we all love to party, but drinking in moderation tends to ensure that we won't say or do anything that we'll regret in the morning.

8. When with someone, make sure you introduce him or her to the person you begin a conversation with. It is best to do this early on, before the fact that you haven't already done it becomes awkward.

9. What if you don't know or can't remember someone's name that you've been talking to for fifteen minutes? As hard as it might seem, it is best to own up to it right away: "I'm really sorry, but I forgot your first name." ("Jim.") "Jim, this is my wife, Betty." Potentially uncomfortable? Yes, but the alternative of trying to fudge the situation could be a lot worse.

10. Many people try to come up with really interesting things to say to keep a conversation going. That's a lot of pressure. Instead, work harder at really listening to the other person. You will wind up picking up several interesting points that you can follow up on with a question or comment of your own.

11. Keep the business talk to a *minimum*. Even though you are in conversation with people with whom you want to do business, that doesn't mean you have to exclusively talk about business. Sometimes you can actually hurt yourself with a client or a prospective client by talking too much about business. Give it a break. Most of us already work fifty or more hours a week. There are so many other topics to

discuss. Now if *they* bring up business, that's a different story.

12. This might sound like a contradiction, but if you are invited to a cocktail party of a prospective business client, make sure you know who the key players are and a little bit about them. Do a little research. Find out where they went to college, where they live, and maybe a bit about their family (only if this information is easily attainable). It makes it so much easier to break the ice and make casual conversation.

13. What do you do when you are in deep conversation with someone and someone else you know (and might even want to talk with) interrupts you and starts a conversation? Two options. You could politely say, "Hey, Bob, great to see you. This is Jerry Smith. Jerry, this is Bob Jones. Bob, I'll be with you in a few minutes . . ." and go back to your conversation with Jerry. Another option is to bring Bob into the conversation; "Hey, Bob, great to see you. This is Jerry from the Turner Company. We were just talking about the World Series. . . ." It really comes down to whether you want Bob in the conversation. The key is to know you have options.

14. Speaking of interrupting conversations, it can be particularly awkward to enter a conversation even if you know one of the parties involved. In most cases, you shouldn't barge into a conversation in progress, particularly one that seems pretty intense. But if someone's body language sends the message that it's a light conversation and that they might be open to others joining, then go for it. According to Susan Roane, author of a great book titled *How to Work a Room,* "If you merely want to extend a greeting to someone in conversation, you might say, 'Excuse me for interrupting, but I wanted to say hello' and then move away. You may find your interruption is a welcome relief and that you are invited to stay and chat."

15. Now comes the hard part. The key to getting out of a cocktail party conversation gracefully is once again knowing you have options. You could excuse yourself and say you have to go to the restroom, or go with the standard; "It's been great

talking to you, Mary, but I think I'm going to get myself a drink." Or, "Mary, it's really been great speaking with you, but I see someone I haven't spoken to in years. Take care of yourself."

The key here is to be direct without being rude. Some people will bend your ear all night if you let them. Don't let them, unless you really want to talk to Mary all night. If you want to mingle, then mingle; it's expected that your conversations will last between five and ten minutes and then you move on.

Don't you just love the holidays?

Motivation

Chapter 64

"YOU HAVE TWO WEEKS: TICK-TOCK"

Sometimes it's not just the message you send, but the vehicle you use to send that message that can wreak havoc on an organization. E-mail definitely has its place in the modern workplace, but as a tool to lead, motivate, and potentially threaten large numbers of employees, it can be a disaster waiting to happen. Take the case of Neal Patterson, Chief Executive of the Cerner Corporation, a software company based in the Midwest with about 3,000 employees. Recently, there was a published report about Mr. Patterson's communication faux pas when he attempted to get a message to about 400 of his employees regarding his desire to get them to work harder and for longer hours. Look at his e-mail and decide how you would have felt being on the receiving end:

"We are getting less than 40 hours of work from a large number of our 'employees.' The parking lot is sparsely used at 8:00 A.M., likewise at 5:00 P.M. As managers, you either do not know what your EMPLOYEES are doing, or you do not CARE. You have created expectations on the work effort, which allowed this to happen inside Cerner, creating an unhealthy environment. In either case, you have a problem and you will fix it or I will replace you. . . . You have two weeks. Tick-tock."

This message from this corporate leader is a classic example of how NOT to use e-mail. Not only were large numbers of company employees confused but they were peeved. Further, word of Patterson's angry e-mail found its way onto the message board at Yahoo!. Within three days

Cerner's stock price fell approximately 25 percent. There was chaos in the company, which could all be traced back to an effort by a leader to increase "productivity" by getting people to respond favorably to his electronic threat. The real problem, however, is that Neal Patterson is not alone. There are thousands of corporate executives, managers, and administrators who use e-mail to send controversial and potentially misunderstood e-mails to large numbers of employees that wind up only making things worse within the organization. Of course, Mr. Patterson was later quoted as saying that he was taken out of context and that Cerner employees misunderstood that he was exaggerating just to make a point. But the fact is he is the culprit; the sender of any communication must be held responsible for the interpretation of it. The sender must work harder to think through how a message (be it sent face-to-face, over the telephone, or via e-mail) will be received.

To test out the Patterson e-mail, I asked my friend Judy, a top-level manager at a New Jersey- based high-tech company, how she would have reacted to such an e-mail from her boss. Judy said, "It definitely would have de-motivated me because I don't like to be threatened. The CEO should have met face-to-face with his top managers at the Kansas City location and discussed his concerns about productivity. Together, they should have come up with a game plan as to how to communicate those concerns and generate further discussion among the employees in question." Finally, Judy added, "Since when are the number of cars in a company parking lot a clear-cut measure of employee productivity? On the *Seinfeld* TV show, George Costanza made an entire career of looking busy at his desk while doing absolutely nothing." Judy's got a point there.

As for Neal Patterson, he is quoted as saying his e-mail was intended to "start a fire" but instead he "lit a match, and started a firestorm." He adds that he wished he had never hit the "send" button on this most destructive e-mail. Final piece of advice: It's not a bad idea to have a trusted colleague or friend read such a sensitive e-mail and get some honest feedback before you decide what to do with it. Like a lot of technology, e-mail can be great, but only when used correctly.

Chapter 65

A PAT ON THE BACK PAYS BIG DIVIDENDS

M ost people think that motivating employees is largely about how much we pay them. This is a simplistic view, which isn't particularly helpful for team leaders and managers who are trying to get the most out of their people in these most challenging of times. First of all, most organizations don't have the money to simply give more to their people. Second, employee surveys have found that at best, money is a short-term motivator, which doesn't compare to a variety of other incentives that matter to most people.

Consider this short list of people motivators:

- Give employees AUTHORITY along with responsibility. It's easy to tell employees they are responsible for accomplishing a particular task or goal. It's easy to say you are going to hold them accountable if they don't succeed. The hard part is giving up control and a degree of authority. A recent Gallup Survey found that 66 percent of employees say managers want them involved in decision-making, yet only 14 percent feel they have been empowered to make those decisions. Something is out of whack. Therefore, it is crucial to give employees the authority to make critical decisions and encourage them to take risks. Having authority empowers people, and feeling empowered is a tremendous motivator.
- People want and need to be recognized. It's no different than when you were in third grade and you received a gold star or had your name prominently listed for some classroom accomplishment. It felt great then, and it feels just as good now. Yet, some managers fail to understand the need to recognize the accomplishments (no matter how small they seem to the managers) of team members. If an employee has done the work on a particular project, put that employee's name on the cover of the project report. If an employee is actually running a program, give that person a title that acknowledges his

or her efforts (director, manager, project leader, etc.). Employee newsletters, whether printed or published electronically, offer another great opportunity to celebrate the accomplishments of employees. Many will hang it in their office, bring it home, tell others, and feel really good about themselves. And feeling good about yourself is a tremendous motivator.

- Don't be so obsessed with trying to catch people doing things wrong that you are blind to when they do them right. Be on the lookout for people doing a good job. It's a question of perspective and attitude. We often see only what we choose to see.

- While private recognition is great, sometimes acknowledging an employee in front of his or her peers can pay really big dividends. Just make sure you spread it around.

- Keep employees in the information loop. Make sure you let your people know about critical organizational accomplishments, challenges, or opportunities. Being informed gives employees a feeling of ownership over the team's destiny. Many managers let their people know only when it is too late. This causes people to feel more like victims than participants. Simply put, being involved and informed is energizing.

- Provide direct, personal feedback to employees as quickly as possible—preferably within twenty-four hours. Most people really want to know what their manager thinks of their work. The more detailed and constructive the feedback, the better. Handwritten comments signed by the manager are usually best, but providing feedback can also be done through e-mail. It's simple, fast, and efficient, yet too many managers miss the opportunity and in turn many of their employees feel ignored. Getting constructive, tangible feedback causes most people to work harder and give more of themselves.

- Other motivators include celebrating employee birthdays, anniversaries, and work-related milestones. In addition, social and recreational activities, including employee softball and bowling leagues, create a sense of togetherness and team spirit.

- Finally, saying "thank you" on a consistent basis really motivates people. It doesn't cost anything, takes little or no time, and leaves a lasting impression.

Chapter 66

"YOU NEED IT WHEN?"

All of us who have projects and deadlines at work have been frustrated by procrastinating peers and colleagues. These are the people that "yes" you to death but just don't get important work done on time. Very often they are nice, pleasant, and you wouldn't mind hanging out with them after work, but boy are they frustrating when it comes to business matters.

With this in mind, consider some tips and tools to help those less than stellar workmates to get the job done in a timely fashion:

- Negotiate a very specific deadline for a particular project. It's better to actually get the other person to come up with a time and a date. For example, "Jim, when exactly will you have the Jones project done?" If Jim hesitates, politely persist, making it clear that an open-ended situation is unacceptable, "Jim, I know you have a lot of items on your plate, but the Jones project is really important. So instead of me setting an unrealistic deadline, tell me when you can get it done."
- It's one thing to have Jim come up with a date, but if that date is unacceptable or simply unreasonable, make it clear to Jim the reason why. "I appreciate the date you have agreed to, but as you know, there are many other projects that will be adversely impacted if we wait that long. So given that reality, let's come up with a compromise."
- Once Jim agrees to the date that works for you and your organization, it is absolutely essential to verbally repeat what has been agreed to: "Great Jim, I am looking forward to receiving the Jones project on September 15. It will be a big help." Then, follow up in writing with an e-mail reconfirming the date.
- Put a little added pressure on Jim by cc'ing key players within the organization, possibly even the president or the CEO. Make it clear to Jim that you have informed others who matter that he has agreed to a specific date and time regarding a specific project. Your objective is to move this from a situation

that involves just the two of you and to ultimately avoid a "he said–she said" type of situation.

- In certain instances, even if a procrastinating colleague has every intention of meeting a certain deadline, he or she may not have the skills or tools to get the job done. Therefore, ask a few questions such as, "Jim, tell me some of the keys to getting the project completed." Then, listen. If it sounds like he is off course, say, "Jim, this sounds great, but you might be better off speaking to . . ." You can save you and Jim a lot of time.

- One of the worst mistakes managers make in these types of situations is to give lazy direction using very weak and confusing language. "Jim, be sure you make the Jones project a priority and work on it any chance you get." When you hear yourself using such language, realize the potential for miscommunication and start getting specific.

Finally, when Jim meets the agreed-upon deadline, make sure you acknowledge his efforts. Tell him face to face and follow up with an e-mail telling him he did a great job and once again copy other key players in the organization. This is about closing the loop and creating what is commonly referred to as a "best practices" situation. It sets the tone for others and teaches Jim powerful lessons not only about getting projects done on time but about how people are expected to communicate in the workplace.

Chapter 67

A RESISTANT AUDIENCE PRESENTS A BIG OPPORTUNITY

Recently, I was asked to give a motivational speech to 500 employees of a corporation that was about to merge with another corporation. Many of these employees would soon be laid off. Others were hanging on to their jobs by a thread, but all were fearful of the change that was about to take place. It was very clear early on that there were pockets of resistance to the idea of an outsider coming in telling those in the company that they needed to have a "positive attitude."

We have all faced audiences that resist or object to what we have to say. How we deal with this opposition will have a tremendous impact on our ability to lead and communicate effectively. With that in mind, consider the following tips to help you deal with an audience that is less than receptive:

> Understand the resistance as a normal reaction to an idea that is new or unfamiliar to your audience. Change is scary. So instead of trying to ram your idea down people's throats, communicate a sense of empathy and appreciation for your audience's concern. Let them know that you "respect their points of view" and then offer a different way of looking at the situation while not discounting them or their opinions.

> Hear the audience member's entire objection or comments about what you've had to say. Don't interrupt the person who is objecting. Very often, the audience member who is resistant wants to be acknowledged and heard and doesn't have anything particular against you or your message. Simply put, don't take it personally.

> Look for an audience member who you believe to be supportive of the message you are communicating. Engage that person in a dialogue and get him or her to express his or her support publicly. What this will do is break down any potential barrier between you and the audience and that "us" and "them" mentality. When resistant audience members can see that their peers are supportive of you, they will tend to be more open-minded as well.

> If an audience member raises an objection and mischaracterizes your position in the process, don't argue or debate. Rather, respectively say something like, "Susan, I can appreciate your point of view and how you have interpreted my message. However, I need to make myself more clear. What I'm really saying is . . ." The key is not to criticize the other person, but rather to recognize the possibility that you have not communicated your

message effectively enough and to see this audience resistance as an opportunity to clarify things and move forward.

If an audience member raises an issue or a challenge to your presentation that you see as valid or legitimate, say so: "Bob, that's an excellent point that I hadn't thought of. I need to incorporate that into the plan. It will make it a lot better. Thanks." What you want to communicate to your audience is that you are open-minded and receptive to other ways of looking at the situation. That will make you more likable and therefore more persuasive.

Try to get audience members to be more specific with their concerns. If an audience member makes a general objection, offer this: "Nancy, I really would like to know why you feel that way. Could you expand on that point?" Often, audience members aren't even sure why they object. By forcing them to be more specific, you may help them see that they really don't disagree with you at all.

Remember, a resistant audience represents nothing more than an opportunity for a great communicator to step up and show his or her stuff. It's all how you choose to see it.

The Customer
Is Always Right

Chapter 68

THE CUSTOMER IS ALWAYS RIGHT

Small things matter. Listen to customers when they tell you what they want. If customers say they don't like tomatoes or onions in their salad or they want dressing on the side, give it to them the way they want it. Did you ever notice that when your meal comes out and it doesn't match what you asked for, the waiter or waitress will inevitably say, "Oh, sorry, I didn't write it down" or "I had it written correctly, I guess the kitchen ignored it." Don't ignore it, because small things matter . . . a lot.

Maintain a positive attitude. Your positive attitude will be contagious.

The opposite is also true. A negative attitude will be picked up right away by customers. If you don't feel good about yourself, it is hard to feel good about the people you are helping.

Don't be afraid of customers expressing concerns or problems they are having with you or your business. Encourage them. This is an opportunity to show how much you really care.

The most irritating thing for customers is when they are made to feel like a number and not a person. Even if you are efficient when dealing with customers, they need to be recognized as individuals. (This is particularly challenging for toll collectors, bank tellers, and telephone operators who deal with dozens, and sometimes hundreds, of people a day.)

When dealing with customers, talk in an easy-to-understand, jargon-free fashion that they won't have to work overtime to comprehend.

Every person in every organization must be involved in identifying, getting, keeping, and putting a smile on the face of every customer.

Ask yourself this question—If I were a customer in this situation, how would I want to be treated?

When a customer is angry or disappointed with you or your company, make sure you LISTEN to his or her entire complaint or objection. Fight the urge to interrupt because you want to "fix" the situation right away. (Customers want to be fully heard.) Provide customer service "better than it needs to be" as opposed to "I guess this is good enough."

Feelings matter a lot in customer service. Price, location, and selection are all important. However, by far the most important factor that determines what kind of relationship you will have with a customer is how you make him or her feel.

Never underestimate the power of a smile and a "thank you."

Your frame of mind is critical. If you see your job as simply a way to earn a living, it is going to be extremely difficult to treat customers in a special way. Customers know when you are going through the motions.

Excuses for not delivering a product or service as it was promised often fall on deaf ears with customers. Barring truly extreme situations or emergencies, all promises to customers must be kept. If they can't be kept, it is your responsibility to communicate that to the customer, not the customer's responsibility to find out after the fact.

Finally, great customer service is not about any campaign or initiative to show that you appreciate customers. Rather, it is a way of life and an attitude that is built into the way you deal with people on a daily basis.

Chapter 69

CUSTOMER SERVICE SHOULD NEVER BE SUBPAR

Jerry Pagano is an educator who spent many years moonlighting as a head waiter in a great Italian restaurant. Jerry is big on interpersonal communication and customer service. He believes you can't provide quality customer service without caring enough to listen to your customer. Jerry is also a golfer who plays on public courses. Recently he had an experience on a public course that provides a graphic example of how not to treat customers.

Jerry says, "The condition of the course and the attitude of those who work there communicated an awful lot about how they view customers." Jerry said the tee boxes and greens were beaten up and not maintained. The water stations had no water, which is kind of rough when it is ninety degrees outside. They had few if any rangers to make sure especially slow players kept moving. A four-and-a-half-hour round wound up taking five and a half hours. When Jerry asked one of the rangers he happened to see if he could try to move things along, the ranger responded, "Who do you think you are?" Jerry said, "I'm a customer. I'm just asking you to do your job." Jerry also noticed that the halfway house (or snack bar) didn't open until 10:00 A.M. However, golfers often begin playing at 6 A.M. So much for customer service. Jerry also said the people behind the counter didn't smile and just took his money without even looking at him. "They really seemed unhappy to be working there."

Jerry's bad experience points out a persistent problem when it comes to how certain organizations fail to see that they are in the business of customer service. It can be a public golf course, the DMV, or a department store chain. You can talk about quality customer service until you are blue in the face (or have the catchiest slogan about how much you care), but if the people in your organization don't appreciate customers and don't want to please them, it's a sham. If employees see those they interact with as nothing but an inconvenience, their attitude as well as their verbal and nonverbal communication will show it.

While this pervasive problem can happen anywhere, it seems particularly bad in the public sector. When was the last time you had to go to a DMV or unemployment office? Did you ever ask yourself why you feel like anything but a valued customer? It's because for the most part, those in charge of these organizations don't see you as a customer. They figure you have no other choice but to be there. What are you going to do if you don't like the way you are being treated at the DMV? Go to a different DMV office around the corner? There is only one.

Much of poor customer service comes from organizational leaders communicating negative messages. If those at the top provide no customer service training or do not monitor their employees' communication style with an eye toward improving it, why should frontline people really care? Employees who go the extra yard with customers need to be rewarded and recognized. Examples of first-rate customer service need to be applauded and modeled. When bosses fail to do this, employees are demotivated. If organizational leaders don't do customer surveys or seek feedback on how to improve these interactions, the message sent is that those things aren't important.

No matter what business you are in, ask yourself the following question on a regular basis: "What message am I communicating both in my words and actions when it comes to our customers?" Ignoring this question is risky indeed.

Chapter 70

"GUERRILLA MARKETING" MAKES SENSE

Virtually every professional is involved in promoting, selling, or advertising something. Put together, these activities come under the umbrella of marketing. A colleague of mine recently described marketing this way: "Marketing is the strategy you apply in order to sell your idea, concept, service, or product to a group of targeted customers."

Even if you don't advertise, you still must have a marketing plan.

And while today's buzzwords around marketing include such terms as branding, imaging, positioning, and synergy, all this comes down to communication. There are countless books, newsletters, and infomercials about how to *sell* more effectively. It's much harder to get quality information around the broader topic of marketing. One of the best books on the subject is called *Guerrilla Marketing: Secrets for Making Big Profits from Your Small Business.* The book's author, Jay Conrad Levinson, has written a dozen books in the "Guerrilla Marketing" series. Levinson's advice is straightforward, sensible, affordable to implement, and relevant to any business or professional. Here are some of the key "Guerrilla Marketing" themes that might be helpful to you:

- Marketing is everything you do to promote yourself and your business. It includes the name of your business, hours of operation, how you package your product or service, and the color and design of your business card.
- Marketing involves such things as how your people answer the phone, follow up with customers, and greet people when they walk in the door. It's also about your presentation to an individual prospect and the personal note you send after the meeting thanking the prospect for his or her time. It's all marketing.
- Clearly, money is a factor in marketing, but unlike more traditional marketing activities that are heavily dependent upon big bucks, "Guerrilla Marketing" is more about how you manage your time, energy, imagination, and resources. For example, you can spend $1 million on a bells-and-whistles, super-slick advertising campaign while the receptionist who answers the phone in your company is rude and unprofessional. It doesn't cost you more to have a good receptionist, but it does require you to take the time to make sure the person in that position has the right attitude and the necessary skills to perform that function.
- While some business experts will tell you that it is essential for your business to diversify, "Guerrilla Marketing" says that you should specialize and narrow your focus in an area that allows you and your organization to stand out among the competition.

- "Guerrilla Marketing" promotes the idea of using a combination of techniques and tools to communicate with existing and potential customers. Some people swear by the Internet as a marketing tool and put all their eggs into that high-tech basket. In fact, in most situations a more integrated marketing approach including a web site, direct mail, advertising, newsletters, personal notes (both handwritten and via e-mail), and face-to-face meetings is usually more effective.
- "Guerrilla Marketing" advocates that while you are trying to bring in new clients, one of the keys to success is to expand upon the business you do with existing clients. The key to achieving this is what Levinson calls "the immense power of customer follow-up and outrageously good service."
- Finally, "Guerrilla Marketing" is about building relationships with people, one at a time. There is no simple or easy way to do this. As Levinson says, this is a "painfully slow process by which you move people from their place in the sun to their place on your customer list, gently taking a grasp of the inside of their minds and never letting go . . . no detail is too insignificant. In fact, the smaller the detail, the more important it is to the customer." Like I said, it's all marketing.

Chapter 71

JACK MITCHELL "HUGS" HIS CUSTOMERS

Hugging your customers. Sounds pretty weird, right? Not if you ask Jack Mitchell, CEO of Mitchells/Richards, an extremely profitable clothing business based in Connecticut, and author of the book *Hug Your Customers: The Proven Way to Personalize Sales and Achieve Astounding Results.* Says Mitchell in his book, he and his family have been "hugging" customers since 1958 and today they do over $65 million in sales. Regardless of economic times, Mitchell's clothing business has done well, and this is largely based on the loyalty it has engendered from customers.

A few years ago, Jack Mitchell decided to sit down and put on paper some of the keys to great customer service. But *Hug Your Customers* is a book about a lot more than customer service. It's about empathetic and highly personalized communication. It's about leadership that comes from the top of an organization and permeates down to every employee.

- Jack Mitchell says you don't have to actually physically hug your customers, although he argues some do want and need that. Rather, it is a metaphor for how people want to be treated. The cornerstone of creating a "hugging" culture is to know your customers. We are talking REALLY knowing them. Knowing about their family as well as their likes and dislikes. Knowing their moods and knowing their business.

- When people say it's not personal, it's only business, a hugging culture says that's bunk. Of course it's personal. Never underestimate the importance of a customer actually liking you on a personal level. In his book, Mitchell calls his customers "friends" and he appears to really mean it. Of course your product or service has to be of high quality, but people buy from other people, and underestimating how personal that dynamic really is can be a dangerous mistake.

- There is no substitute for passion. When things are going badly and sales are down, Mitchell says it's passion and an undying commitment to the customer that has gotten his company through these difficult times. It's a passion that you can't manufacture or fake. It's not simply about greeting customers with a smile and a handshake, it's about actually giving a damn about helping them. While you can train people on some of these important communication and customer skills, the key to building a great organization is to bring people to your team who have the potential to care deeply as opposed to those who are simply looking for a job.

- The real work begins as soon as a sale is made. A hugging philosophy says that as soon as you purchase my product or service, my job is to make sure you are not only satisfied, but really happy with it. That means not waiting too long to reach out and communicate that you want to know how things are going with the customer. Too many salespeople are so obsessed with making the sale that as soon as it's done, they are on to the next prospect.

- Traditional sales and customer service talks about market share and return on investment. The hugging approach believes it is more about customers than about merchandise. It believes that if you are loyal to your customers, they will be loyal to you. It fosters building relationships based on trust and open communication. If you do these things at every level of the organization, in most cases profits will come.

Go ahead. Give your customers a hug. What do you have to lose?

Communicating with
Strength in Tough Situations

Chapter 72

CONFRONTATIONAL AND CONTENTIOUS ARE NOT THE SAME THING

Paul is a thirty-year-old bank manager who is well liked, hardworking, and respected in his company. Yet, recently Paul's CEO suggested some executive coaching as a way to help him take his skills to the next level.

A little background. While no one questions Paul's willingness to work hard and be a team player, he is reluctant to "step up," as his boss says. When pressed by the executive coach, the boss explains that Paul runs meetings that ramble and are unfocused. "He is such a nice guy. He often seems reluctant to cut people off when they are on a tangent." He also says that when Paul's team fails to come to any consensus or decision, he tends to put that same agenda item off until the next meeting. Over time, these less-than-stellar leadership and communication skills have hurt Paul's career advancement.

During a recent coaching session, Paul was asked about these issues. His response is revealing. "I am really uncomfortable confronting people. It is not my style to be in someone's face and I don't like it when people do it to me." As the session continued, it became clear that Paul saw "confrontation" as exclusively a negative communication approach. Along with so many other professionals, this bank manager sees confrontation as a form of aggression, as something that makes people uncomfortable—confrontation as a battle, a contest, a war fought by combatants who will either win or lose.

Clearly, confrontation can be and sometimes is many of these things. But there is another way to look at "confrontational communication" as an opportunity to confront an ongoing problem or challenge head-on. To not confront it would mean missing a big opportunity. How many of us have long, simmering, below-the-surface feuds going on with people we need to get along with? It could be at work or in your personal life. Your bottled-up frustration and anger is making your life miserable and greatly affecting your productivity. In these situations you MUST confront things head-on.

Consider Paul, our bank manager, who needs to say to his colleagues who refuse to reach a decision on a crucial business matter: "Let's be clear, by not coming to a decision on X we stand to lose a lot of potential revenue. If our team is unwilling or unable to decide, I will do it because the alternative will produce an unacceptable outcome."

When Paul was presented with this more direct communication approach by his executive coach, he said, "I can do that! But that's not being confrontational." Yes it is! It is confronting your colleagues (or others) with your candid view of a situation. It's confronting by communicating the consequences of our action or inaction. Confrontation in this form is a critical leadership tool.

On a personal level, I encourage you to confront anyone with whom you have longstanding issues or concerns that are truly bothering you. Why not tell your wife or husband or someone close to you, "When I do something extra special for you, and you don't even acknowledge it or say thanks, it makes me feel really lousy." No malice. No animosity. No rancor or battle to fight. Just honest communication about something that matters. That's right, confronting the issue. Think about it. The alternative of ignoring or ducking the situation only makes things worse and gets you more frustrated.

Chapter 73

GOING BEYOND HONESTY TO EMPATHY

It's good to be candid when communicating difficult or sensitive information, but that's not always enough. Attempting to be straightforward and truthful, an executive might say to a room full of employees, "I want to be honest with all of you without any bologna. About half of you are going to be fired. We are going to give you two weeks full pay and I want your desks cleaned out by Friday." An honest physician might say to a patient, "You have cancer in your liver and only one month to live." Whoa! Clearly, this is not good communication. It falls far short because the conversation lacks the other element that absolutely must be added to the formula for effectively communicating in difficult circumstances—empathy.

I recently conducted a series of focus groups with executives who were changing their organizational structure and laying people off. I asked them, "What do you think the people who are going to be laid off really, really want?" Of course we know they want to keep their jobs, but when that's not going to happen, what do they want next? These execs had no idea. They had a very hard time looking at the situation from the employees' point of view. And that's where the ability to communicate difficult information begins—with taking time to think about what YOU would need to hear in that same situation. I told these company executives to first figure out how they would want to receive the news that they were being laid off. Then I said, "That's the way you have to speak to your employees."

That's what empathy is all about. It doesn't mean you actually put yourself in the other person's shoes, because that is impossible. The business executive isn't the one being laid off. The oncologist isn't the one with cancer. The key to communicating with real empathy is to make the attempt to imagine what it might be like to receive this information. In the vast majority of cases when other people believe that you are making that attempt, they feel appreciative. Again, of course they are not happy to hear the news, but your effort to empathize will make it just a little more bearable.

I know what you're thinking: Imagining what it might be like to be in another person's shoes is very difficult. But, I came across a book recently called *The Art of Winning Conversation*, written by Morey Stettner. Stettner says one way to be more empathetic is to practice visualization, which he argues is "using your imagination to see. This process involves replacing your personal frame of reference with another." Stettner says taking such a mental leap requires detachment so you can gain an objective view of how you communicate and how others respond.

Remember, empathy, when communicating in difficult situations, can't turn your words into words the person wants to hear. But you can deliver the facts in a way that acknowledges that this is a human being you're talking to—someone with feelings and needs. No one knows this better than Dr. Elissa Santoro, who is a surgeon trained in oncology. Dr. Santoro cares for women with breast cancer. Here is what she told me recently: "I have spent seventeen years at the bedside of people newly diagnosed, being treated, and dying and they taught me that what they wanted was inner peace. The cure was not the issue—it's the whole person that wants to be healed."

Dr. Santoro's insightful analysis applies to many life circumstances. The people you are talking to may know you can't change the facts and "cure" them, but they can expect you to talk to them with sensitivity, understanding, and, yes, empathy so they can more easily accept the bad news and move toward "healing" that part of their life.

Beyond all the tools, techniques, and takeaways this or any other chapter in this book offers, sometimes what communication comes down to is simply treating another person like a human being. And sometimes that is easier said than done.

Chapter 74

"THE CHANDELIER IS PERFECT— FOR THE WALDORF!"

Recently my wife, Jennifer, and I got into a heated argument about a chandelier she purchased for our home. When she asked me how it looked, only half in jest I said to her, "The chandelier is perfect . . . for the Waldorf!" I was trying to communicate that the chandelier was simply too big for the space. She got somewhat defensive and said that since I wasn't especially involved in household issues before, it was unfair for me to be so critical, especially since the chandelier was special-ordered and could not be returned.

At this point, I was getting a little annoyed and said I thought she didn't handle the situation very well. Then I made this communication faux pas: "If I were handling this, none of this would have happened." At that point, she got very defensive (justifiably) and said, "Fine, then you handle the house from now on. I quit!" I angrily responded, "You can't quit. I can't quit my job just because things get a little rough."

Fortunately, such conversations are rare between us, but you get the idea. We were having a dumb yet heated argument about a chandelier. We were both in heavy "argument mode" and weren't listening to one another. It was only when our one-year-old starting making funny faces and laughing that the tension subsided and we finally both broke out laughing, realizing the absurdity of the situation.

But there is a bigger lesson in all of this, including what happens when we get into "argument mode." Disagreements are clearly inevitable between people that spend a lot of time together. Yet, arguing rarely produces a positive outcome for either party. When was the last time you felt better after a heated argument with someone in your family or at work? It just doesn't happen.

Following are some reasons that arguing is such a destructive communication approach:

- When in argument mode, we aren't likely to listen to or care about what the other person is saying. That is a dangerous place to be. We can become mean-spirited and very competitive. We become obsessed with "winning." As Deborah Tannen says in her book *The Argument Culture* (Ballantine, 1999), "You use every tactic you can think of—including distorting what your opponent just said—in order to win the argument." Simply put, arguing is polarizing.

- We often say hurtful things that we don't really mean. The problem is that once these things are put on the table ("You are such a jerk," or "The way you handled this was really stupid"), it is hard to take these words back, even after you apologize. People you care about get wounded and hurt. These wounds sometimes take a long time to heal and cause irreversible rifts in meaningful relationships.

- Anger puts people on the defensive. Participants feel compelled to protect themselves. By communicating in such an aggressive fashion, the argument only ratchets up. Alternatively, some people decide they are not going to fight back, so they shut down emotionally and intellectually.

- When you argue too often with those around you, it devalues your point of view. You can be seen as a person who flies off the handle at the drop of a hat. When a real circumstance arises that you want to debate, your voice will become muted.

- When we fight, we are not likely to accept or acknowledge a legitimate point raised by the other party. Finally, when arguments go too far, you can't even remember what you were arguing about because things are spiraling so out of control.

Next time you are tempted to go into "argument mode," ask yourself whether you are prepared for these and other negative consequences. I wish I had done this when it came to that stupid (OK, OK—not so stupid) chandelier.

Chapter 75

"YOU'RE SUCH A JERK" AND OTHER INSULTS

"You are such a jerk. I don't know why the boss keeps you on the payroll." "You'll never last here. You just don't fit in." "You look terrible in that dress. Have you gained weight?"

Insults. We've all been the target of them and most of us have hurled them at others. But how exactly do we deal with being insulted? In most cases, when someone says something nasty and hurtful to us, we stew privately and maybe complain to friends and colleagues about it. ("How could Liz have said that to me? We've worked together for ten years and I've always been so supportive of her. I can't believe it.")

But, what does that really get us other than angry and resentful? Rarely do we deal in a constructive and coherent fashion with nasty comments that are directed toward us. Yet, the ability to do this is an extremely valuable communication and life skill.

With this in mind, consider these tips and tools you can use the next time someone takes a shot at you:

- Don't take the bait. Many times, people insult you just to see what your reaction will be. They want to get into an argument. It's to their advantage to get you to stoop to their level. Consider some options that will keep you on the high road: "Bob, you have a right to your opinion, I just don't see it that way." Or, "Jane, I'm not going to get into a shouting match with you. It's not constructive." Your objective is to diffuse the situation and to communicate the message that you are not going to play this counterproductive game. Often, the other person will feel stupid for saying something so hurtful and hopefully lighten up.
- Ask the other person to elaborate on his insult. "Bob, I'm not really sure why you are saying that, but I want to understand. What exactly have I done that would cause you to call me such names?" Your objective is to force the person to back up his charges and move beyond the name-calling.

- Tell the other person how the insult makes you feel: "Jane, when you scream at me in the office, it tells me you don't respect me or my work effort. Is that your intent?" YOUR intent is to put up a mirror to your coworker and ask her to take a close look at her behavior and the impact it is having on you.
- Humor can help. Sometimes you can just kind of shake your head, roll your eyes and say, "Come on, Bob, you can't really mean that. I know you love me anyway, so I'll ignore what you said." This has the potential to make light of an unfounded insult: however, the other person can perceive that you are patronizing him. Be prepared for that possibility.
- Don't let yourself be abused. It's one thing to use communication techniques to diffuse the situation, but that doesn't mean you should allow yourself to be consistently ridiculed. If you try these techniques and the other person continues to insult you, consider removing yourself from the situation if at all possible. Life is too short to spend an inordinate amount of time around people who are consistently negative.

Finally, the worst thing you can do is to hurl an insult back in an effort to defend yourself or let out frustration. Doing this may make you feel better in the moment, but it is guaranteed to create a downward communication spiral.

Chapter 76

THE REAL "NO SPIN" ZONE

"Mets Blow It Again. Announce Piazza Will Begin Shift to First—before Telling Him" *(New York Post)*

Consider an example from the world of baseball on how not to communicate. This is a story about the New York Mets and their star player Mike Piazza, whose days as a catcher appeared to be numbered and who was expected to one day be playing first base. The lesson is relevant for any professional who must communicate difficult news to an important team member for the overall good of the team.

There had been talk about Piazza playing first base for years. His legs are old, his arm is tired, and his bat is more valuable to the Mets if he plays the less strenuous position of first base. (Managers regularly consider who on their team should be playing what position at a certain time based on a variety of factors.) Yet, Mets management apparently was reluctant to talk directly to Piazza about the move. They allowed the media and the rumor mill to drive the situation, thereby causing them to lose control. Piazza was constantly asked by the media about the move, but he responded that the Mets leadership had never spoken to him about it.

Well, the Mets did what so many organizations do. They stuck their head in the sand hoping that a nagging problem would magically go away. That's poor leadership. Wishful thinking is no substitute for the hard work of strategic planning and communication. A critical component of any leader's game plan should be the willingness to make tough decisions and in turn communicate those decisions to those who need to know about it—BEFORE someone else tells them.

When confronted by the media, who had been tipped off by someone in Mets management about the move, Piazza was taken aback and stated in the *Star-Ledger*, "We all got to get on the same page. I told them I would do whatever needs to be done for the organization." It shouldn't have been that hard to get on the same page on such an obvious issue. Airing your dirty laundry is embarrassing. Yet, communicating with a key player like Piazza through third parties was unacceptable and created unnecessary turmoil and resentment within the organization.

What the Mets should have done is broach the subject with Piazza in the off season (timing matters), when both parties could look at the situation with more perspective. Being up-front and candid with Piazza about the move to first base may have angered him, but it would have allowed him the time necessary to come to grips with the issue. It would have also allowed all parties to communicate a united front and allowed Piazza to gradually and gracefully gain the skills and tools necessary to move into the new position.

Again, this story has little to do with baseball or sports. It's really about the need for managers in any organization to communicate honestly about what must be done for their team to succeed. Change is hard, but sometimes it's essential. Great managers don't simply ACCEPT change, they LEAD and EMBRACE it. They communicate with passion and compassion about the need for change. They don't hide or duck the tough situations. They step up and are accountable. When these things are done, even though there will be some pain, there is a greater chance of success. The New York Mets missed a golden opportunity to demonstrate real leadership when it really mattered.

Chapter 77

THE FEDS ARE NOT ON THE SAME PAGE WITH THE ANTHRAX SCARE

Since September 11, 2001, the information communicated by numerous public health professionals and government officials has often been confusing and contradictory, particularly when it comes to anthrax. Clearly it's not an easy job to communicate to an especially anxious public in the midst of a terrorist threat—real or perceived. While this case involves government professionals, the lessons here are relevant for professionals in any field.

In a time of crisis, it is critical to speak with one voice, one message, coming from one primary executive in charge. Yet, from the beginning, Health and Human Services' secretary Tommy Thomson was saying that we were "prepared" to deal with any biochemical warfare. Others in the federal government were telling a very different story. Thomson, who often seems nervous and uncomfortable in press conferences, said there was no reason to worry about anthrax when the first victim, photo editor Bob Stevens, got the disease and died. He kept saying the case was "isolated" and did not involve any "evidence of terrorism." A few days later, Attorney General John Ashcroft told a different story. "We don't have enough information to know whether this could be related to terrorism or not." Further, Ashcroft said there was a "clear criminal investigation" going on. Two high-ranking government officials with two very different messages.

The anthrax sent to Senator Tom Daschle was described by an assistant secretary of defense as "run of the mill" anthrax. Yet, a day before, a top general investigating the Daschle anthrax said it consisted of "pure spores." Translation: this could be deadly stuff. Was it "run of the mill" or was it "deadly"? Sure, you can only deal with the information you have at the time, but public health officials have a responsibility to communicate in a clear, understandable, timely, coordinated, but most of all accurate fashion.

Another problem involves the use of language. When Tommy Thomson says the federal government is "prepared," what does that really mean? Prepared for what? What exactly does it mean when the FBI tells us to beware of any "suspicious looking" packages or envelopes in the mail? Some other words that are confusing—you are "probably" not at risk, or we "believe" there is not a problem. These words and expressions are left to one's interpretation or imagination. Qualifiers like "probably" and "believe" are confusing. The messages sent to postal workers regarding the safety of their workplace was very different from the message sent to congressional staff members as it relates to anthrax. Federal officials communicated that virtually everyone who worked at the Capitol should be tested for anthrax and many were put on antibiotics. Postal workers, many of whom were in areas where anthrax-laced letters passed through, were told not to worry, to go to work, and that there was no need to get tested or go on antibiotics. All that changed after several postal workers got anthrax and two of them died. Different messages communicated to different audiences about the same issue.

Finally, the public had this situation to deal with—Postmaster General John Potter said that "the threat is in the mail . . . there is no guarantee that the mail is safe." Yet White House spokesman Ari Fleisher said on the same day that Americans shouldn't worry because the mail is "overwhelmingly safe." You're kidding, right?

Again, government officials have an incredibly difficult job to do in these pressure-filled days. Mistakes are bound to happen—but not at this rate. Much of the problem is a product of a sloppy, uncoordinated, and unprofessional communication strategy. Important information is not being shared with those who need to know. Let's just hope it gets better from here.

Chapter 78

A RESPECTFUL "NO" HELPS BUSINESS GO

Saying "no" or rejecting someone's idea, proposal, or advice seems simple enough, but for many on both a professional and personal level, effectively communicating what seems to be a simple "no" can be complicated. With this in mind, consider the following tips on being clear for saying "no" while minimizing the fallout.

- Sometimes people say "no" with a negative attitude that sends the message that they simply don't care. Unless that is your intent, don't do it. Remember, you can disagree without being disagreeable. You can say "no" and still have some empathy and compassion.

- Some people think that when they say "no" they have no responsibility to explain themselves. Rarely is this the case, particularly when you are dealing with people you DO care about regarding an important business or personal matter. As parents, when our children ask us why the answer is "no," we often say, "Because I said so." You may get away with this approach with kids, but as a manager it is not going to work. Your "no" should sound something like; "Mary, your proposal to redesign the office has merit. But after considering the cost, the timing isn't right. But I appreciate your effort." Remember, you are saying "no" to the idea, not to the person.

- A "no" doesn't always have to be communicated right on the spot. There is nothing wrong with saying, "Joe, you've given me a lot to think about. That's exactly what I am going to do and we will talk tomorrow." Buying time to think through an issue is fine, but don't use this approach to procrastinate and avoid making a tough decision. Sooner or later you are going to have to respond, and the fear of saying "no" shouldn't get in the way of you being the leader you are expected to be.

- What happens if someone isn't listening when you are saying "no" or if people bring up other points to make their case? If any of these efforts are compelling enough to have you change your mind, then do it. However, if your answer is still "no," just use the "broken record" approach: "Jim, I appreciate what you are saying, but rearranging my schedule to attend your event isn't going to work." Be respectful and remain calm no matter how many times the request is made.

- When saying "no" you should consider if there are alternatives that haven't been put on the table: "I'm not able to sign on right now, but I can recommend a colleague who might be able to help you." Or, "I can't meet with you on the 17th, but if there is any way you can do it the day before, we could work something out." The point is, "no" doesn't always have to be an unequivocal "no," particularly when dealing with someone with whom you want to continue a positive line of communication.

- While e-mail, telephone messages, and other electronic communication mediums may be the EASIEST way to say "no," sometimes the most effective and respectful approach is to say "no" in person. The other party may still be disappointed, but is likely to appreciate the personal touch.

- Finally, "no" sometimes has to mean "no." Make sure you leave no confusion as to what your intent really is. The worst thing that could happen is to have someone walk away from a conversation thinking there is still a chance you might say "yes" when in your mind it is just not going to happen. Saying "no" doesn't make you a bad person.

Simply put, saying "no" doesn't have to be so difficult, particularly when you consider that you have more communication options than you might have originally thought.

Chapter 79

HOW TO DEAL WITH WORKPLACE BULLIES

Bullies come in all shapes and sizes. As parents, we worry that our kids will be picked on by the bully in school. We also hope that our kid won't become a bully. Funny thing is, bullies aren't only kids. We all know bullies, and others who get bullied, in the workplace.

Recently, my nine-year-old son brought home a great book on the subject entitled *Bullies Are a Pain in the Brain,* by Trevor Romain. The book is largely about how to communicate with bullies and minimize their negative effects. Romain also offers a range of practical advice and tips that are useful not just for our kids but for professionals who feel they are being unfairly picked on by people they work with and for. Consider the following:

- When dealing with a bully, your body language matters a lot. Bullies tend to target those with poor posture, downcast eyes, and a drooping head. If your nonverbal communication says that you are confident about yourself, bullies aren't likely to pick on you. So stand up straight and look people in the eye. If you act more confident, you actually begin to feel more confident.

- Most of us feel ashamed or uncomfortable to admit that we are being bullied. First, acknowledge that it's not your fault that you are being bullied, it is the bully who has the problem. If you are being bullied at work tell coworkers or tell your supervisor. Bullies don't want to be exposed for what they are. The more support you can gather among others, the harder it will be for the bully to isolate you for more abuse.

- Confront the bully who consistently says mean things to you. ("Hey, Bill. Why do you even come to work? You are never going to be promoted.") You don't have to fight the bully, but make it clear that you are willing to stand up for yourself. Look the bully in the eye and say; "Hey, Sam, lay off. I'm not interested in what you think." Or, "I don't like what you are saying. I'd appreciate it if you would stop." You don't have to yell it. The key is to let the bully know that what he is doing is unacceptable.

- But weren't we taught that if you ignore the bully he will go away? Sometimes they do, particularly if he can find another target. But in the book *Bullies*, Romain says, "Some bullies may get more angry if you ignore them . . . they may keep provoking you until they get some kind of reaction." While ignoring the workplace bully is an option, it's not a particularly good one. Bullies are looking for control and power. If it's clear that you are not willing to give it to them, you become a less attractive target.

- Role-play or rehearse how you are going to deal with the bully. Don't assume that the words, body language, and demeanor will all come to you in that critical moment. Like most communication challenges, dealing with bullies is a matter of practice. Look in the mirror, pretend you are talking to the bully, and say what you need to say. Better yet, ask a friend or family member to stand in for the bully and play the whole thing out. It will help to get you in a better, more confident frame of mind.

Bullies are everywhere. They can be bosses, coworkers, colleagues, and spouses. If we can't help ourselves deal with bullies, how are we supposed to help our kids?

Chapter 80

SWEATING IT OUT AT FOX

A while ago, I appeared on the Fox News Channel program *The Big Story* to offer analysis on how the media were covering the Laci Peterson murder and the Kobe Bryant sex scandal. I had done this kind of work countless times, and public communication is my business.

But as I was sitting there waiting to go on, I started to feel a bit anxious, even nervous. I wasn't exactly sure where this was coming from. Then all of a sudden I felt a bead of sweat on my forehead. Oh no! Then, a really bad picture came into my mind. It's that dreadful scene in the movie *Broadcast News* in which reporter Albert Brooks finally gets his big chance to anchor the network news and he starts to perspire. He sweats so much because of his nervousness that they have to change his shirt during a commercial break. This was not a smart image to have in my head.

From experience I realized that the key was to quickly get my body and mind under control. As I sat there waiting for the segment, I realized that part of the anxiety came from just sitting there waiting and thinking about what could possibly go wrong. Instinctively I started a conversation with one of the technicians about the Kobe Bryant case and we got into an interesting dialogue. As we talked, my heartbeat came down, as did my anxiety level. Within seconds, I started to feel in control again.

The point is, regardless of how experienced we are in communication, we can all feel some degree of anxiety and nerves in certain situations. It could happen before a big speech, a job interview, or a meeting you have to run. It could also happen in a sporting event; for example, professional golfers who miss a two-foot putt when the championship is on the line.

Regardless of the situation, the following techniques will help get your nerves under control so you can perform under pressure:

Put down the coffee. Sure, caffeine might pump you up and give you some energy, but it is going to also trigger your nervous system and potentially get your heart racing, which produces a lot of bad stuff.

Breathe. Force yourself to breathe in through your nose and out through your mouth. Sounds stupid, right? But when we get nervous we sometimes forget to breathe evenly. The key is to develop a rhythm to your breathing, which will in turn slow your heart rate, thereby centering you.

Use your nervous energy. This can mean moving around a bit, getting into a conversation with those around you, or shaking your arms and hands. The key is to expend your nervous energy in a productive way. If not, it gets bottled up and manifests itself through "cold sweats," dry mouth, and really weak knees.

Focus on your message. Concentrate on what you want to say or do and why it is important to your audience. Remind yourself that the reason you are asked to be in this situation is because you have earned this right based on past performance. Say to yourself, "I've been here before and I can handle this."

Know that nervousness is natural. Don't try to fight it. Yet, don't obsess over it. Accept that nerves are part of the process of getting ready to perform. Trust that it will go away as you get into the moment. Then you will actually find yourself enjoying the experience, which will remind you why you are in this situation in the first place.

Remember that you are not alone. You are not the only one who gets nervous, anxious, or scared. Even the best communicators experience it at one point or another. You are in good company. No, you're not perfect—none of us are!

Chapter 81

DON'T PLAY WORD GAMES WHEN APOLOGIZING

If saying "I'm sorry" is so easy, then why do so many people have such a hard time doing it? How do you apologize effectively and have the offended party forgive you? Consider the highly publicized apology of U.S. senator Bob Torricelli after the Senate Ethics Committee "seriously admonished" him for his dealings with discredited businessman David Chang.

The Torricelli debacle in many ways is less about politics than it is about what people expect of their leaders, be they in government, business, or the nonprofit sector. Most people expect their leaders to be decent, honest, and ethical and willing to admit when they've messed up. Given the recent rash of corporate scandals, these particular leadership qualities are more important than ever.

As a senator, Bob Torricelli was an excellent communicator and a compelling public speaker, but apparently he and other high-profile figures such as Tyco's Dennis Koslowski, Enron's Ken Lay, or even publicist Lizzie Grubman haven't figured out how important the truth is when things go wrong. For months Torricelli insisted that he never took any "gifts" from David Chang, except most people would call a big-screen TV, CD player, and jewelry for which you don't pay full price a "gift." Finally, when the Ethics Committee concluded that Torricelli did in fact take gifts from Chang, Torricelli offered this less-than-genuine apology: "I agree with the Committee's conclusions . . . fully accept their findings and accept full responsibility." But then Torricelli added, "It has always been my contention that I believe at no time did I accept any gifts or violate any Senate rules." Give me a break. Lots of problems with that "apology":

- When apologizing, you can't wait too long to do it. Torricelli did. Don't wait for someone else in authority (i.e., your boss) to say you did something wrong. It's best for you to proactively admit your mistake and apologize immediately.
- When you apologize, don't offer explanations or caveats. It makes the apology ring hollow. In Torricelli's case, he said he agreed with the Committee findings but then reasserted that he did nothing wrong. Well, which one is it? Apologies shouldn't contain mixed messages.
- Torricelli also said that he was sorry because his "interpretations [of Senate rules] were in error." Huh? Be sorry for taking gifts that you weren't supposed to take. How else could you have "interpreted" getting free stuff you didn't pay full price for? Don't play with words. (Think of Bill Clinton parsing around what the "definition of *is* is" when talking about his interpretation of "sexual relations.") As a recent *Star-Ledger* editorial stated, "Senator Torricelli engaged in a hopeless semantic dance intended to make this sound like a small technical matter."
- Disclose early and honestly. Technically, Senator Torricelli didn't have the authority to release the transcripts from the Ethics Committee. However, he could have aggressively pushed the Committee to disclose the documents. His stance? "I don't

think I am in a position to contradict them." Again, technically, the senator was not in a position to contradict the committee, but if great leaders really want people to know the full truth, they would not cling to technicalities. They push for what is right, especially when people still have more questions.

The bottom line is whether you are a U.S. senator, corporate executive, high school teacher, spouse or child who has done something wrong or broken the rules, the way to say "I'm sorry" is pretty much the same. And since we all mess up more than we'd like, the lesson Bob Torricelli learned has value for the rest of us.

Note: This column was written before Bob Torricelli was forced to drop out of his reelection campaign in 2002.

Chapter 82

BUSH'S BLIND SPOT

One of the most important attributes of a great leader is the ability to admit his or her mistakes. Since leaders are faced with so many problems and challenges and are in a position to make countless decisions (or avoid them), things inevitably go wrong. Mistakes are made. The sign of an evolved leader is not that she avoids making any mistakes; it's that when she does, she admits them and learns from them.

That's why it was so disturbing that during the 2004 election President George W. Bush was either unable or unwilling to acknowledge a singe mistake he has made in office. The first time he was asked publicly about his mistakes was by John King of CNN at a press conference. The president appeared stunned by the question. He was clearly uncomfortable. Finally, after hesitating, he said he wished he were "given that question beforehand." He strained a bit more and added that "he was sure he could come up with one mistake," but that it was "difficult to do under the bright lights and the pressure of the situation."

As he spoke, the president was rocking back and forth, looking around the room and up at the ceiling. It was hard to watch. Since then, I've used video of the moment in numerous communication and media seminars to demonstrate to clients how *not* to handle a difficult question.

A few months later, in the final weeks of the campaign, the president was asked the exact same question by a citizen in one of the debates. Again, he couldn't (or wouldn't) acknowledge a singe mistake. In both instances, President Bush looked like an inept public communicator.

The lesson here is about how people in positions of power communicate about their errors in judgment or miscalculations and what they (and their team) can take from them. The lesson is about how a leader can use the same mistake as an opportunity to show both vulnerability and strength at the same time. It's about how President Bush and so many leaders have apparently not learned this important communication lesson.

The irony is that some leaders see admitting mistakes as a sign of weakness. (I'm sure Bush's advisors told him this. They were dead wrong.) Acknowledging errors and committing to improve has the potential to strengthen our relationships with colleagues, stakeholders, as well as family and friends. According to Mike Krzyzewski, Duke University basketball coach and author of the book *Leading with the Heart*, "When a leader makes a mistake and doesn't admit it, he is seen as arrogant and untrustworthy. And 'untrustworthy' is the last thing a leader wants to be."

That's why Krzyzewski and other smart leaders are so willing to admit their mistakes. They understand the heavy price you pay when you don't do it. It's not as hard as you think it is. Admitting your mistakes communicates that you believe in the relationships you've developed. People around you need to know that you are human. They need to know you have the trust in them and in your own leadership to say, "I'm sorry. I didn't handle XYZ well. I take full responsibility. Here's what we need to do to get things right and back on track. . . ."

Or, conversely, say, "I know there is a lot of finger-pointing going on about why we didn't meet our desired goal, but I'm the team leader, therefore, I take responsibility. But as a team, we need to get this right. Rob, what one thing do you believe we need to do to meet our target?" The constant is acknowledging responsibility. The variable is whether you give clear direction on how to proceed or ask for input from others.

What is so hard about communicating in this fashion? Is there any risk to doing it? Sure. But there is a much greater risk in not acknowledging that key stakeholders perceive that you are refusing to take responsibility for a particular mistake.

So ask yourself, "How often do I acknowledge my professional mistakes?" If the answer is "not often," what is stopping you?

Chapter 83

LESSONS FROM THE MCGREEVEY RESIGNATION CRISIS

Jim McGreevey's story is a sad one. He will always be remembered as the youthful-looking governor from New Jersey who was forced to resign after appointing his gay lover to head up the state's homeland security after 9/11. Interestingly, two memorable speeches will serve as bookends over those tumultuous few months of McGreevey's tenure. The first was his "I am a gay American" speech on August 12, 2004, in which he said he would resign. This speech was covered by every major television and radio network as a major news story. The second was McGreevey's "swan song" speech on November 8, 2004, in which he tried to put some context to his life in public service. It received a lot less coverage.

"I Am a Gay American"

I can't imagine what was going through Jim McGreevey's mind as he stood before a gaggle of microphones and cameras on that fateful day under those awfully bright lights and announced his resignation. Even though his wife Dina and his parents stood by his side, McGreevey looked very much alone. That is because McGreevey alone was responsible for the amazingly poor judgment in appointing Golan Cipel, who he had met in Israel and had an extramarital affair with, to head up homeland security.

Let's be clear—I couldn't care less what Jim McGreevey's sexual orientation is or isn't. That's his business. And I have little tolerance with people who are quick to judge other people's relationships. Keeping our own together is challenging enough. Yet, McGreevey's cardinal sin was to allow his sex life to cross over into his public life. Golan Cipel was in no way qualified to head up homeland security, especially after 9/11. Mc-Greevey had to know that, but he was blinded by love or lust—who knows? After a barrage of criticism, McGreevey dropped Cipel's nomination and appointed him to the position of "special counsel" to the governor at a salary of $115,000 of taxpayers' money. Another bad move. McGreevey made it worse by his overly defensive communication strategy of keeping Cipel shielded from the media and refusing to go into details as to what Cipel's responsibilities were.

The way McGreevey handled the Golan Cipel stuff was bad enough. Add to that numerous scandals and corruption investigations of Mc-Greevey's top aides and major fundraisers, and the foundation of his administration was crumbling around him as he stood there announcing his resignation. With his voice shaking, he said, "I am a gay American." These words were carefully chosen. Not gay, but a "gay American." Mc-Greevey is the son of a hard-nosed and notoriously strict father who was a marine drill instructor. It was as if the governor had to demonstrate some form of patriotism and loyalty to flag and country while announcing he was gay. Oddly, he had to "play it straight" right up until the end. Under this unimaginable pressure, McGreevey delivered what would be his most effective speech in his twenty-year career.

He wrote the speech himself and knew exactly what he needed to say. He was composed, but wasn't afraid to show the powerful emotions he clearly was feeling. He didn't mince words, he was direct, and the vast majority of those who heard his announcement, whether they liked the governor or not, had to be impressed. If we had had more of this Jim Mc-Greevey early on, things might be very different today.

After the announcement, McGreevey went underground. He refused to speak to the media (I tried several times to schedule an interview with the governor through his top aides). He moved about his business with heavy security around him, keeping away anyone who might ask an embarrassing question. This looked silly. Aggressively avoiding cameras and reporters sends all the wrong signals. It says you have something to hide and that you are not confident.

"I Am Sorry—So, So Sorry . . ."

McGreevey emerged on November 8, 2004, to deliver his farewell address. This time he stood there alone. No family with him. His parents were not feeling well and who knows if his wife Dina could stand being put through this again. There were just a few oversized photos of McGreevey's better days in office that served as a backdrop. The governor's speech was short—only fourteen minutes. It was emotional and well received by the approximately 400 cabinet members, supporters, and longtime McGreevey loyalists in attendance.

Within the first few minutes, McGreevey declared: "I am sorry—so, so sorry that mistakes in my judgment made this day necessary for all of us." After apologizing in several different ways, McGreevey went on to talk about what he was most proud of. Nice stuff, but most people watching on TV probably weren't sold in the way those in attendance were.

On a personal note, it was extremely sad to watch this relativity young man in his mid-forties walk away in disgrace. McGreevey and I are the same age. We met when I was a twenty-six-year-old legislator and he was a twenty-six-year-old legislative aide who made it clear that one day he wanted to be not just governor, but president. Twenty years later his political career and his reputation were in shambles. Whether you agree or disagree with his policies, there was something terribly sad in all this.

So what can the rest of us take away from the McGreevey debacle in terms of leadership and communication skills? The biggest lesson is about full disclosure. Disclose quickly, totally, and don't play games. Take the advice of your lawyers, but don't be a slave to it. Of course people embroiled in such a controversy are concerned about future disclosure and how what they say could be used in court. However, these concerns shouldn't stop those under pressure from being forthright, candid, and confident if they truly believe they are doing the right thing and that what they are saying is true.

The other lesson is to admit your mistakes and take full responsibility with no excuses or caveats. To his credit, Jim McGreevey has done that even though many questions still remain. The other lesson is to be totally honest with both your family and your closest advisors. They can't really help and support you if you leave out certain embarrassing details. Of course this is easier said than done, but the alternative only invites more problems. The cover-up is always worse than the crime.

The biggest lesson may be that any of us at any time could find ourselves making a terrible decision or using really bad judgment and then find ourselves in really hot water. Fortunately for most of us, when this happens it doesn't play out on such a public stage. But regardless of what arena you are in, the rules for communicating in a crisis are pretty much the same.

Finally, while we are all complex human beings, no one can succeed if there is such a dramatic disconnect between the person we are at the core and the person we purport to be in public or professional life. Of course, we all have secrets—embarrassing things we have done or said, and would be hurt if anyone else found out. Ironically, maybe the only chance Jim McGreevey had to succeed in public life was to proactively tell his own story, but tell it a lot sooner instead of when his back was against the wall and he was allegedly being blackmailed by Golan Cipel and his attorney. McGreevey spent his entire public career trying to tell people what he thought they wanted to hear. Interestingly, what he needed to tell us most was the truth, as painful as that may have been. He opted for a different communication strategy and paid the ultimate price.

Chapter 84

MARTHA WHIPS UP REAL THIN IMAGE SPIN

At the time that Martha Stewart was convicted and sent to jail in 2004, beyond all the legal and criminal issues facing the domestic diva, she had a huge challenge ahead of her in the effort to restore her reputation and gain the public's trust. She embarked on an aggressive media and communication strategy in which she portrayed herself as a victim who had done nothing wrong. Said Stewart, "After more than a year, the government has decided to bring charges against me for matters that are personal and entirely unrelated to the business of *Martha Stewart Living Omnimedia*. I want you to know that I am innocent—and that I will fight to clear my name."

I've got to believe this proactive communication strategy has the approval of her lawyers as well as her high-powered public relations experts. Yet, while going on the offensive does make some sense, there are several flaws in this strategy. The biggest problem is that Martha Stewart's message is not especially believable or credible.

Remember when Martha Stewart went on the *CBS Morning Show* right after the scandal broke? She insisted on chopping lettuce for some sort of Fourth of July salad, stating, "I think this will all be resolved in the near future and I will be exonerated from this ridiculousness. . . . We are going to make salad." The image of Stewart chopping lettuce while insisting that she was innocent created a really weird picture. The messages sent were confusing at best. Her nonverbal communication was saying, "I'm really uncomfortable with all this, but I'm trying to keep up a strong front." Months later, Stewart apparently still didn't get it.

When Stewart was lead away from a federal courthouse, she was surrounded by a team of lawyers and bodyguards immediately after her indictment. This communicates not only that you are embarrassed, but you might have something to hide. What Stewart should have done was hold a press briefing where she made a clear and confident statement looking right into the cameras directly to her audience watching at home.

However, when it comes to communicating any message, the first and most important criteria is this: Is the message credible or believable? If the answer is no, virtually nothing else matters. It doesn't matter how much money you spend to get the message out or how many times you repeat the message. If you and the message are not seen as truthful, you might as well forget it. That's Martha Stewart's biggest problem. Most people don't believe her story that she just happened to sell her ImClone stock the day before a very negative FDA report about one of ImClone's drugs became public.

Assuming you are willing to acknowledge that you made some mistake or did something wrong, here are a few ways to communicate that message:

- Communicate quickly before others expose your wrongdoings. Every day you wait to admit you were wrong reduces the chance of any public understanding or empathy.

- Apologize to anyone who has been hurt by your mistake, particularly your customers and stakeholders who have invested in you and your organization based on their belief that you would do the right thing.
- Don't offer detailed explanations or excuses for what you did. No extenuating circumstances or crying the blues about your terrible childhood.
- Take full responsibility for your actions without blaming others, even if others contributed to the mistake or problem.
- Don't quibble over the details (like Bill Clinton debating the dictionary definition of "sexual relations"). Lawyers too often play word games that may be helpful in the court of law but become problematic in the court of public opinion.

It may be too late for Martha Stewart, but it's not too late for the rest of us who make mistakes every day.

Chapter 85

COMMUNICATION CRISIS FOR THE CATHOLIC CHURCH

The Catholic Church has become the latest poster child for how *not* to communicate in a crisis. Thanks to Church leaders' inept handling of the ongoing pedophilia problem among certain priests, Enron and Arthur Andersen have gotten some breathing room.

The question of how to communicate when you or your organization has clearly done something wrong is addressed elsewhere in this book. The *Harvard Business Review* has dozens of case studies on crisis communication. Yet, officials in the Church have ignored the most fundamental rules of communication and are clearly paying the price.

The first rule of communicating in a crisis is to act quickly and decisively without mincing words. However, it took the Church too long to acknowledge that there was a problem with certain priests who had sexually abused children. Further, because the Church took so long to go public, it appeared that Church leaders didn't acknowledge the seriousness of the problem and were not that anxious to do anything about it.

The next rule of crisis communication is to speak in a unified voice with a clear and credible message. That's not what happened here. While the Pope is supposed to be the CEO of the Church, what he was saying on this issue was often contradicted by individual bishops. Some Church leaders said they would turn over any priest who was accused of sexual abuse to civil authorities. Others said they would continue to handle the issue internally and only disclose the name of an accused priest when they thought there was "credible" information. Mixed and contradictory messages in a time of crisis produce nothing but more problems and confusion.

When in a crisis, it is important to be proactive (as opposed to reactive) in your communication, which often allows you and your organization to set a context for the public debate instead of allowing your critics to do it. The Vatican as well as diocesan officials expressed concern for assaulted children only when case after case was exposed in the press. Not only did the Church fail to show enough concern and empathy for the victims (another must when your mistakes have caused innocent people to suffer), but it engaged in scapegoating and blame-shifting. Church leaders implied that they were being victimized and targeted by the media, who they said were exaggerating the problem.

Another important rule is to not let the lawyers control what you say in public. Lawyers are obsessed with limiting liability and preventing possible jail time. Lawyers advise their clients, be it the Catholic Church, Arthur Andersen, Enron, or Bill Clinton, to be less than candid using vague and ambiguous language. They argue about things like the definition of "sexual relations." They play word games. The problem with this legal strategy is that most people know that something went wrong and that someone must be held accountable. Lawyers often tell their clients not to apologize in public. That's terrible advice. The Church should have started apologizing fifteen years ago on this issue, but apologizing in a crisis isn't enough. The key is to acknowledge responsibility and make a commitment to take clear, corrective action to rectify the situation. The longer it takes for you to do that, the bigger the hit you are going to take in public.

Bottom line? Catholic Church leaders have only one choice. Disclose, acknowledge responsibility, apologize to victims, and pray that Catholics and others are willing to give them a second chance.

Chapter 86

DOCTOR, DOCTOR, GIVE ME THE NEWS

For physicians, one of the most difficult aspects of dealing with patients involves communicating news that is less than positive. Simply put, how does one communicate "bad news" to a patient who is anxious, nervous, and downright afraid?

Doctor-patient communication is in many ways the most important aspect of delivering superior healthcare. Sure, the best medical technology and research has its place, but healthcare is largely about human interaction between patients who are sick and physicians who are expected to have all the answers but clearly don't. This chapter is intended not only for physicians who want to communicate more effectively, but also for the rest of us who are healthcare consumers who must interact with physicians and other medical professionals. It doesn't necessarily have to be the way that it is. Doctor-patient communication can be a lot healthier, even in an age of managed care. With that in mind consider the following communication tips, particularly for physicians who have to deliver "bad" news to their patients:

Find a comfortable and appropriate environment to give the test results. Too often, medical information is communicated on the fly or in the hallway of a hospital or doctor's office. Medical professionals should do everything possible to avoid this. Hearing bad news is hard enough, much less having to hear it in front of an audience.

Make yourself available to patients, understanding that they will be extremely anxious until you speak with them. The key here is to build in enough time to allow for an honest and thorough discussion with your patients. In the world of managed care this is easier said than done, but it is an absolute *must* in building rapport with patients and gaining their confidence.

Present your information clearly, with the least amount of medical jargon. Simply put: speak in everyday conversational English that people can understand. Use analogies and examples that patients will relate to. Remember, your patients weren't sitting next to you in medical school and there is no reason to think they understand medical vernacular.

Empathy is king. One of the best ways to communicate to a patient is to imagine what it might be like to be a patient (and everything that entails) and communicate accordingly. This isn't true just for physicians but for anyone in the service or helping professions.

Offer patients other resources to obtain information about their medical situations. A physician can help a patient become his or her own best advocate. However, that can only be done by obtaining accurate and relevant information concerning the illness, diagnosis, or procedure in question.

Be aware of your body language and what it communicates to the patient. Sit at the patients' level and try to avoid looking down on them. Make steady, focused, but relaxed eye contact. This does not mean staring and making your patient even more uncomfortable.

Take the opportunity to touch your patient's hand, arm, or shoulder if you sense that it is needed, wanted, and/or appropriate. You would be amazed at how many patients comment on the "warmth" of a physician, largely because of this personal, soothing, very human contact.

When dealing with certain patients who are often ignored or discounted (for example, children and the elderly), make sure you talk directly to them and not exclusively to the family member or significant other who is accompanying them. All patients want and need to be acknowledged. They also need to participate directly in their own care.

Physicians have an incredibly difficult job these days. Then again, so do patients. It is easy to point a finger and blame the medical community for being insensitive and uncaring, but that won't get the job done. Like all professionals, physicians need help improving their communication skills. By being more aware and informed as to what good doctor-patient communication looks like, we can be part of the solution instead of contributing to the problem.

Chapter 87

WHAT'S UP, DOC?

This book talks about the importance of great communication in customer service, team building, sales, and leading an organization. Every professional, whether an accountant, lawyer, or clerk, must be a first-rate communicator in order to connect with their audience of one or one thousand. One area where excellent communication can literally become a life or death issue involves physician-patient relations.

There is a scene in the movie *Patch Adams,* which stars Robin Williams playing a doctor in training, where a woman who is ill is being wheeled from the operating room by a very detached physician and his residents. The physician begins touching her and talking about her using medical jargon as if she is not even there. When the physician asks, "Any questions?" Patch Adams responds by asking the patient, "Yeah, how are you doing? I'm Patch Adams, what's your name?" The physician reprimanded him for asking the patient's name and said, "You need to stay detached from the patients because you'll deal with so many of them who will probably be gone in a year or two. You don't want to lose all that emotionally."

Do doctors and healthcare professionals need to be detached because they deal with so many patients? To get some answers I recently spoke with a group of physicians and other healthcare professionals regarding the essence of doctor-patient communication. Here are some excerpts from that discussion:

Dr. Arnold Gold, professor of pediatrics and neurology at Columbia University and founder of the Englewood Cliffs-based Arnold P. Gold Foundation, promotes humanism in medicine and the concept that physicians need to look beyond science, medicine, and technology in order to truly provide quality healthcare to their patients.

Dr. Gold says, "Communication training and truly listening to patients are integral parts of medical school education. This is a part of an ongoing process in the educational development of a physician-in-training and a medical student as well as the residents. For example, a caring, compassionate physician who is communicating in a very personal manner is demonstrating the importance of caring and is a role model for students and residents."

Dr. Steve Miller, Director of Pediatric Emergency Medicine at New York Presbyterian Hospital, believes, "You can't turn every physician into an outgoing and social individual. However, there are certain things a physician can do to convey warmth and understanding. Take, for example, the golden first minute when you first meet a patient. I teach medical students to keep this first interaction with a patient very open-ended and allow the patient to really talk, while prompting him or her to say what's on his or her mind."

This theme of listen first, talk later is a critically important tool that helps break down barriers and creates a more open and supportive environment. This approach helps not only in doctor-patient communication but in any interaction in both professional and personal situations.

Dr. Adrienne Headley, a faculty member at Robert Wood Johnson Medical School, stresses the importance of empathy in doctor-patient communication. "I think empathy is putting yourself in the patient's shoes by trying to imagine what they might be feeling. Once I approach a patient from that vantage point, the emotional distance is minimized. I'm still a professional and I am going to offer my expertise, but I also realize that we are both human beings; we are both reaching out to each other, and that the patient needs my help."

Dr. Headley also shares her views on the concept of humanism in medicine. "We are human beings before we are physicians. The best doctors never lose sight of that fact. The best doctors always keep in mind that we all at some point have to interface with our mortality."

What is there left to say? The humanism in medicine movement makes a lot of sense. What profession couldn't use a little more humanism?

Relationships, Kids,
and Communication

Chapter 88

COMMUNICATING WITH OUR KIDS

Some kids are better communicators than others. Did you ever notice that certain children look you right in the eye, speak in a clear voice without rambling, and do it with genuine enthusiasm? What makes other kids mumble, look down at the ground, and rock back and forth when they have to speak? According to Dr. William Sears, a pediatrician of thirty years and the author of the book *The Successful Child*, the way children communicate is largely a product of how their parents communicate. Dr. Sears says children are the world's best copycats, and communication skills are more commonly caught than taught.

Don't kid yourself. Being a solid communicator is as important to kids as it is to adults. Kids who can express themselves confidently are better at building solid relationships. They perform well in school and later on are better able to find a good job and a good mate. Dr. Sears argues that there are several things parents can do to help their children master the art of communication without being overbearing or obsessive.

- Narrate your life even when interacting with an infant: "Mommy (or Daddy) is taking off your diaper and cleaning your bottom so you can have a nice clean diaper." As children get older, parents should describe such things as the items they need to pick up at the grocery store or what they see on a walk in the park: "Aren't the trees beautiful?"

- Be a great listener. I know many children who are terrible listeners, who also have parents with the same problem. The key is not to tell your kid to listen, but to actually practice being attentive and empathetic when conversing with your own child. Avoid the temptation to interrupt your child even when he or she is going on. It's a lot better to wait for a pause in the conversation and then divert the attention to another subject.
- Ask the "W" questions. Instead of asking closed-ended questions such as, "Did you have a good day at school?" which only elicits a yes or no response, ask more open-ended questions that often begin with "who," "what," "where," or "why": "What did you do at school that was really interesting today?" When your child responds, use encouragers like, "What happened next?" or "Tell me more."
- Don't nit-pick about communication or grammar mistakes. Dr. Sears says, "It is important for kids to learn to speak comfortably before they learn to speak correctly." I was guilty of correcting my son's grammar as far back as preschool. The problem with that is, even though we are all tempted to do it, sometimes kids can clam up or develop speech problems because they feel as if they are being judged. Look, grammar is clearly important, but kids need to first figure out how to express what they are feeling, thinking, or seeing, then we can help them fine-tune it.
- Also, remember that body language counts a lot. We can say all the right things to our kids, but if we do it while rolling our eyes, crossing our arms, or our slumping shoulders, the meaning of those words will be interpreted very differently. When talking with or listening to children, Dr. Sears suggests we get down to their level and look them in the eye. Imagine what it must be like to talk to someone who is four feet taller than you are. That's got to be weird. Just crouch down or even get on the floor if you have to. There is no substitute for eye contact. Not only will it help you connect with your child, but it will teach him or her what eye contact should look like.

Chapter 89

HELPING OUR KIDS STAND AND DELIVER

Many adults have problems and issues with having to get up and speak in front of others. This book covers that topic in a variety of ways. But before most of us became adults who felt anxiety about public speaking, we were kids that experienced the same thing.

Recently, my son's sixth-grade teacher asked me to come in and coach her students in preparation for their first oral presentations of the school year. In many ways, coaching kids is not very different than coaching adults. But if you can get kids to think of public speaking as something that doesn't have to be painful, the possibilities are endless.

So if you want to help your child get a head start in the communications game, consider the following tips for kids who have to "stand and deliver."

1. Know your main message, which is the most important point you want to make in your presentation. If you haven't figured this out, neither will the other kids. They may forget some of the details of your presentation, but your point should be easy for the other children to understand.

2. Get to the point. You should be able to state your main point in twenty seconds or less. Think about how quickly you get bored when another student is going on and on.

3. Think about what YOU would want to hear if you were in the audience. Try to imagine your presentation from the point of view of the other kids. Do you want to hear lots of confusing statistics and facts that mean little to you? Neither do the other kids.

4. Instead of reading every word of a speech you have written out, make an outline of key words or phrases to keep you on target. Doing this will help you be more conversational and relaxed.

5. Make sure you keep your eyes on the students in the audience. Look each one individually without staring. (That

would look really weird, wouldn't it?) Don't just look at the teacher or your best friend in the front row. And whatever you were told about focusing on a spot on the wall above the heads of the other kids—forget it. That looks even weirder.

6. Think about the boys and girls in the back of the room and make sure they can hear you. So, SPEAK UP! Don't shout, but project your voice and go slow.

7. Stand up straight, but don't be stiff. Watch that rocking back and forth. And your feet shouldn't be crossed, they should be firmly on the ground. Try to move around a little bit instead of just staying in the front of the room. I know it is a little bit scary at first, but you'll get used to it.

8. Use your hands to make a point or to gesture. That's what they are there for. DON'T put them in your pockets. DON'T play with your hair. DON'T be fumbling with your papers or your jewelry.

9. Get into the presentation instead of just "getting it done." DON'T fake it. Show your enthusiasm for your topic. The other kids will like that. If you are having fun, so will they.

10. Practice your presentation in front of your family and do it the way you plan to do it for real. The more you practice, the more comfortable and confident you will be when the time comes to "stand and deliver."

Chapter 90

COMMUNICATING WITH KIDS ABOUT A SCARY WORLD

The World Trade Center and Pentagon attacks, beheadings in Iraq, children murdered en masse in Russia—communicating with our kids about terrorism, war, and violence, particularly since 9/11, has not been easy. Most of us are unclear about how much or how often we should bring these issues up. Should we bring them up at all? Should we wait for our kids to raise these sensitive and scary topics? What if they don't? Many children have experienced emotional problems since September 11. How honest should we be about terrorism in general and our own fear in particular? Could it happen again? So many questions, so few answers.

With all the media coverage of horrific terrorist and war-related events, consider some practical communication tips when talking with your kids:

- Timing matters a lot. Timing is always an important factor in how and when we communicate. If your child brings up any aspect of war or terrorism, seize the opportunity to hear him or her out. Most parents know that it is better to have a meaningful conversation with our kids earlier in the day or at dinner as opposed to right before they go to bed. Talking about scary, real-life events when both you and your child are tired is not a good idea. However, if your child *does* want to talk before bedtime, seize the opportunity.

- Ask open-ended questions. Instead of putting pressure on yourself to lecture about the nature of war and terrorism, put yourself in listening mode. See yourself as more of a facilitator asking probing, but sensitive, open-ended questions that encourage your children to talk about their feelings, fears, and concerns. Right after September 11, the Mental Health Association published a list of great questions that can help get your kids talking. These questions are helpful after other high-visibility events as well:

  What do you remember about what happened on September 11?

  What have you talked about in school?

  How do you feel about the way our country responded?

- Don't try to do it alone. Place a call to your child's teacher or to school administrators to get a better sense of how they are dealing with highly publicized terrorist incidents. What forums are they providing for kids to talk and share their feelings? If you have a sense of what the school is doing, it makes your job a little easier when talking with your own child on the subject.

- Television communicates a powerful but sometimes distorted and overly scary message. I know because my oldest son, Stephen, who is twelve, watches the *Today* show every morning before school. Even that program shows incidents involving "scary" news. The Mental Health Association advocates that we monitor our children's television viewing surrounding war and terrorism-related stories. TV is obsessed with graphic pictures. Think about the horrific visual of the planes going into the World Trade Center and the towers ultimately collapsing. It is up to us as parents to communicate with our children that such horrific events are clearly not the norm even though we are seeing them again and again. That's what TV news does. It covers rare and unusual events without putting them into context. We need to explain that to our kids.
- Use age-appropriate communication. A five-year-old is not a ten-year-old. Try to empathize as much as possible with how a child of whatever age might be dealing with all this. Then, remember how hard it is for you to deal with this stuff.

Finally, if at times the challenge is simply too much, none of us should ever hesitate to reach out for professional help. To that end, check out a great web site at www.scholastic.com, which helps parents and teachers communicate more effectively with their kids.

Chapter 91

MANAGING ANGER IS BETTER THAN YELLING

Recently, I profiled Yankees manager Joe Torre as someone who seems to handle difficult situations in a calm, supportive, and rational fashion. This chapter deals with anger. It is meant for all of us who have to work extra hard on being more patient and not overreacting to the daily problems, challenges, and screw-ups that are bound to occur.

Managing anger is something I have worked on for years. As a manager, colleague, friend, and father, I have been known (on what I hope are rare occasions) to blow up and say things I immediately regret. Sure, I apologize right away, but those apologies can fall on deaf ears if you keep up the same bad habits.

Let me share a recent incident. Something happened in our office in which a mistake was made on a project. When I realized it, I started asking accusatory questions: "Who's responsible for this"? "How could this have happened?"

When one of my staff members pointed out that getting angry and pointing fingers wasn't going to solve the problem, I still didn't let it go. I hung on to it: "Yeah, but what would have happened if I didn't discover the problem? How many other mistakes are there that I don't know about?"

Luckily, such scenarios are few and far between. Yet one of my colleagues later told me how much that incident negatively affected the morale of our hardworking and dedicated team.

"The staff was really upset," my colleague told me. "They are working their butts off and you made them feel as if you didn't appreciate their efforts—that you didn't trust them."

Ouch!

Over the past few months I have made an even more concerted effort to understand why some of us overreact to things. One of the books that has been especially helpful is *Don't Sweat the Small Stuff* by Richard Carlson. Do yourself a favor and pick it up. It's an easy read, and it's really practical.

Carlson talks about adopting a solution-oriented, problem-solving attitude rather than nurturing a finger-pointing, who's-to-blame point of view. Think about it. The blame game is so counterproductive. It unnecessarily puts people on the defensive and creates bad feelings. It also makes your team members (or others in your life) reluctant to come to you with a problem for fear that you will shoot the messenger.

The more you adopt a "how can we fix it?" attitude, the faster you will reach resolution. The best part is that you will do this without bloodshed. You will also foster an all-for-one, one-for-all esprit de corps.

Another technique for becoming more patient Carlson advocates is to be aware of how quickly our negative thinking can spiral out of control.

"The more absorbed you get in the detail of what is upsetting you, the worse you feel," he writes. Carlson calls this the snowball effect of your thinking. The key is to catch yourself before this happens—before the negative momentum builds.

Very often we blurt out our first thought. If we give ourselves a moment or two to think through what's really at stake, we tend to soften our verbal response. By doing this, we begin to see that the latest office problem or screw-up isn't a matter of life or death.

Chapter 92

ARE YOU A SNIPING SPOUSE?

Anyone who is in an everyday relationship, either at home or in the workplace, understands how easy it is to get into stupid arguments. Sometimes these arguments seem to have no beginning or end. Other times we aren't even sure what we are arguing about. Nowhere is this communication dilemma more real than between spouses. I've seen it with good friends who are couples that seem to be at each other's throats all the time. They nit-pick and criticize one another. They embarrass each other in public. They are reluctant to admit their role in contributing to escalating the argument. They say really mean things when pushed against the wall.

With this in mind consider some ways to avoid becoming a sniping spouse or combative cubicle-mate:

- Because of the need to be right becoming more important than a desire to get along, we can get caught up in arguing our point of view as if we were in a court of law and had to convince some judge or jury. But in any important relationship, being right is overrated. If your goal is truly to get along (and be happy) then a more cooperative, less adversarial mindset is required.

- Don't be so quick to react to what you perceive as the *tone* of the other person. When you do this, you run the risk of misunderstanding the underlying message he or she is trying to communicate. Of course tone matters (which is why you should be aware of your own tone), but we often incorrectly perceive the other person's intent when we look for the worst.

- Avoid complaining about your spouse to friends and family. We all do it to one extent or another. Recently, my wife, Jenn, overheard me complaining to my mother that she wasn't being particularly understanding of my long work hours. Good thing my mother knows how great my wife is and how much of a baby her son can be. Yet, the problem is we sometimes build a case against our spouse (again to make ourselves appear right) and leave out important details to put an argument in context. It's unfair to your partner, and the feedback you get from family and friends is often skewed based on the information you give them.

- Another mistake is to bring up past events. Say you are talking about your partner coming home late without calling and instead of responding to what you have said, he blurts out, "But what about the time YOU came home late without calling?" The intent here is to take the attention off ourselves and fight back. The impact is to build barriers and cause your partner to be less than candid about things that bother him.

- Stop and ask yourself, "What is really bothering me? Why am I so upset about this?" Sometimes it has nothing to do with the person, the situation, or the topic being discussed. It is really about you. Something you are upset with yourself about or some guilt or anger you feel. The key is to look inward first. Check yourself and where you are coming from, because I assure you the other person doesn't have a clue.

- Don't take the bait. It's like a fish that gets hooked. Once you are hooked, it's hard to get free. Same thing in relationships. There is bait all over the place. See it for what it is. Sometimes when you don't take it you can avoid a bad situation. Also, be more aware when you're using bait to catch your spouse.

- When in a "spirited" conversation, fight the urge to interrupt just because you have heard something you don't like. This causes your spouse or colleague to get frustrated and in turn interrupt you. It's a destructive communication pattern that can get out of control. Patience and better listening are valuable tools in any relationship.

- Avoid "I hate when you always ..." and "You never ..." phrases. We tend to use words like "always" and "never" when describing what bothers us about our partner or colleague. People react more to the "always" and "never" reference as opposed to the specific issue we are concerned about. Try to stay focused on the issue or question that concerns you.

Chapter 93

WOMAN EXECS MORE EMPATHETIC? THINK AGAIN

We've all been trying to make sense of this most recent wave of corporate executives acting badly. The president and Congress can do all they want to change certain laws regarding what corporations are required to report, but ultimately much of this corporate ethics problem comes down to leadership or the lack thereof. What causes corporate executives to be to be less than honest, likely to blame others, unwilling to listen to "bad news" from those who work for them, and ultimately to be insensitive to the pain they've caused to innocent people?

In a *Star-Ledger* Op-Ed, an article contributed by *Washington Post* reporter Paul Farhi explored why it is that women in corporate America appear more likely to be "whistle blowers" exposing bad corporate behavior. Is there something inherently different about how men and women manage and lead in difficult situations? In general, are women basically more honest than men? Are they more comfortable with criticism and do they empathize more with those who have been hurt by corporate greed and/or misbehavior?

Stephanie Smith (a pseudonym to protect her) has been a corporate lawyer for fifteen years and has worked with and for men and women in very senior leadership positions. While none of this is an exact science, the experiences of corporate veterans is valuable. Says Stephanie, "Overall, the women in corporate America that I've dealt with are straighter shooters than men. They are more direct, they are better team players and they don't have to always have the spotlight on them." But what about the issue of honesty? Stephanie argues that there was and always will be a good ol' boys network in corporate America. Her sense is that men are obsessed with being part of the "in crowd" and are deathly afraid of being left "out." She says women never feel that they are "in" even in the highest corporate positions. Therefore, she says, "men are less likely to admit that there is a problem. They become 'yes' men."

Stephanie described several women who she has worked with who tried to report corporate wrongdoing and paid a heavy price. One woman, a vice president of operations at a major corporation, was privy to a series of fundamental accounting and corporate governance problems within the organization. She very much wanted to tell the CEO and CFO what she thought was wrong, but according to Stephanie was afraid of losing her job. Ultimately, she took an early retirement package even though she was only in her early fifties. This was top management's way of getting her out of the way and ignoring this very serious internal problem. That company's stock has dropped over 75 percent in the past three years.

So what about the issue of empathy? She says women, in general, have more empathy for those who are hurt by corporate shenanigans. As she was saying this, she stopped and said, "Wait a minute, I'm not so sure about that." She remembered several women executives who she felt were pretty mean-spirited and downright hurtful to those around them. Then she said, "On second thought, I think this one is more of an individual personality trait and isn't all that gender-related."

Is Stephanie Smith right about the leadership styles of men and women? In general, if women were the CEOs in corporate America, would they be more honest, ethical, empathetic, and decent than men? Or, is it something about being the CEO or other top corporate executive that encourages someone to become an out-of-touch, insensitive liar regardless of gender? This is something to think about.

Chapter 94

EVEN CASUAL FLIRTING IMPLIES A SEXUAL AGENDA

Men and women use flirtation as a powerful form of communication in the workplace, whether it's to obtain a job, move up the corporate ladder, or simply get on the boss's or client's good side. But is flirtation between the sexes in and around the office simply innocent and inconsequential, as many men and women want to believe? Dr. Patricia Kuchon, professor of Communications at Seton Hall University, doesn't buy it.

Dr. Kuchon specializes in communication between the sexes and says, "Flirtation is the use of communication for a sexual agenda on the part of the man or woman doing it. If one uses language (written, verbal, or body language) to communicate sexual thoughts or feelings toward another person in a work environment, that is flirtation and in my opinion does not belong in the workplace."

Some might argue that Professor Kuchon is taking too hard a line and that if the parties doing the flirting are comfortable with this form of communication, then it is a nonissue. But according to Dr. Kuchon, flirtation and sex cannot be separated. She calls flirtation "one step in the sexual agenda process" and "the bottom rung of sexual harassment." What she and some other gender communication experts argue is that if you are flirting with someone in the workplace, you have a sexual intention. And unless there is agreement that a sexual encounter is the goal of both parties, flirtation is a very risky and potentially destructive form of workplace communication.

But what about women, and to a lesser extent men, using their "sex appeal" as part of their overall presentation in the workplace? Isn't it true that in certain professions, particularly sales, how "attractive" we are to a potential client or customer has a significant impact on our ability to make a connection and ultimately succeed?

Dr. Kuchon believes that this fact of business life is an unfortunate and often ignored problem, particularly for women working in once-male-dominated workplace situations. Consider the case of Judy, a highly articulate professional who is the marketing representative for a midsize company. "Some men will call and be very flirtatious over the phone. I remember this one guy Jim, who when I told him my boss would get back to him later in the day he said, 'I would rather speak to you than anyone else in the company' and proceeded to shamelessly flirt with me. Was I bothered by it? A little, but the fact is our company needed Jim's business and as long as he didn't say anything that *really* went over the line, it was no big deal. Plus, I'm used to that kind of flirtatious communication from men."

Judy's situation is by no means isolated. It's not an accident that many companies employ attractive young women as receptionists in law firms, PR agencies, and other businesses.

Many women in business will say they "use their sexuality" to gain an advantage with men. I know of several women in pharmaceutical sales who say their communication and sales approach with male physicians is significantly different from how they deal with female physicians. Anything wrong with that? According to Pat Kuchon, the answer is, "Absolutely!"

"Some women use sexuality to move themselves forward. If that is the only way they move themselves up, that is very dangerous."

Complicated stuff. For women, regardless of their position, when it comes to the flirtation game, the operative phrase is "proceed at your own risk."

For men using flirtation as a communication tool, consider this: You better be damn sure that the woman involved is totally comfortable with it and is willing to put it in writing. Otherwise, you could find yourself being accused of sexual harassment and contributing to a "hostile work environment."

Chapter 95

GENDER COMMUNICATION IS NOT SO CLEAR CUT

Imagine you are delivering a speech on the issue of leadership to a women's business group. You are sharing observations about the differences between men and women when it comes to management and communication styles. Your analysis centers on a variety of commonly held beliefs regarding women being more empathetic, better listeners, and more collegial. You say to the group that women in top positions often have a level of sensitivity and compassion that too many male executives lack. You add that men tend to be more aggressive, action-oriented, and more comfortable with confrontation when communicating with their direct reports.

Just then a woman in the audience who is a top executive raises her hand and says, "Frankly, I have found women a lot harder to work for than men." The speaker asks, "But what about all that talk about women sticking together in the workplace and there being some sort of sisterhood among women?" She immediately responds, "That's a joke!" The room erupts with laughter. The speaker (this writer) is perplexed.

Now consider the case of Rosie O'Donnell, the very successful entertainer/entrepreneur who was involved in a contentious court case regarding her now-defunct magazine *Rosie*. Much of the trial centered on O'Donnell's less than rosy personality as a top person at the magazine. In the trial, she was accused by Cindy Spengler, an executive for her magazine's publisher Gruner + Jahr, as saying, "You know what happens to people who lie. They get sick and they get cancer." O'Donnell was characterized as being a mean-spirited manager who often ridiculed her staff and led in a dictatorial fashion. Even if some of this is true, this characterization flies in the face of what many believe to be the "natural" leadership and communication traits of women in business.

So what's the deal? Do men and women in leadership positions communicate in dramatically different ways? Are those differences based largely on gender or does it all come down to the style of the individual leader?

After speaking with numerous men and women in leadership positions, I've come to these conclusions:

- The stereotypes of male/female communication styles are becoming more and more dated and obsolete. The lines are more blurred and the gender picture more complex.
- More and more women lead and communicate in an assertive and in some cases aggressive fashion, often utilizing an "in your face" style. These women can no longer be called the exception.
- Conversely, there are a lot of men in positions of authority who consistently communicate in a compassionate and caring fashion. Again, their approach is shaped less by gender and more by personality, previous experience, and individual philosophy.
- When managers like Rosie O'Donnell allegedly communicate to individual employees like Cindy Spengler in a condescending and personally offensive fashion, such behavior should be examined in a gender-neutral fashion. If true, O'Donnell's communication approach in this instance tells us virtually nothing about women and how they lead, but a lot about Rosie and what she needs to work on.
- Calling people names or yelling in the workplace is wrong no matter who is doing it, and those of us in leadership positions who make this mistake shouldn't use gender as a crutch. Simply put, it is no more acceptable for a man to do this than it is for a woman.

Chapter 96

CRYING HAS NO PLACE IN BASEBALL OR BUSINESS

I've believed for a long time that there are some basic differences in the way men and women approach things, and one of the biggest issues is tears. I work with a great team of talented producers, most of whom are women. Recently, we had a problem that wasn't being handled in the most effective fashion, and I expressed my displeasure about the situation and in the process of doing that I raised my voice in an aggressive fashion. I made it clear that I was very unhappy with the performance of a particular producer, who happened to be a woman. I said, "This is totally unacceptable. Frankly, this is bullshit. Now what are we going to do to fix it? Now!" In the midst of my mini-rant, the young woman started to cry. That wasn't the first, second, or third time that I had seen women crying in a professional situation.

Sorry, but I just don't think it is appropriate. The places where it is appropriate for a woman to cry are the same places that it's appropriate for a man to cry—around a particularly emotional, sad or happy, situation. But no matter how much encouragement, training, and education that women get, there are still a fair number of women in business who cry when challenged in an aggressive fashion in the workplace by either a man or a woman. One can say as a manger you should never challenge in an aggressive fashion, but sometimes it happens.

Do you remember the scene in the movie *A League of Their Own* about a women's baseball team? Tom Hanks, the manager, is yelling at one of the women about making a particularly stupid mistake. The woman begins to cry on the steps of the dugout. Totally exasperated, Hanks says, "Don't you know there's no crying in baseball?" The only acceptable time to cry in baseball is when you win or lose the World Series. You don't cry when your coach is yelling at you or if you strike out.

The Carly Fiorina's of the world (recently ousted CEO of Hewlett Packard) and other women who head up huge organizations are great role models. Fiorina would not cry because someone confronted her in a meeting, or she wouldn't be where she is today.

Ironically, back in 1972, presidential candidate Edwin Muskie's campaign collapsed because he cried at a press conference after a political opponent said critical things about his wife. Not good. No crying in baseball, in business, or in politics. You can cry on election night because you won or lost. But you can't cry in politics because someone criticizes you or your wife.

With all this said, I still believe there should be no crying in baseball or in business, except in those rare circumstances previously described. I know that some people are going to disagree with what I'm saying, but I've seen it too many times to ignore this important workplace issue. It's still hard for many women not to show their emotions on their sleeves and create unnecessary problems. On the other hand, some men can be tone deaf to how their overly aggressive communication can impact others. I don't expect this phenomenon to change anytime soon. You can't say that there's no crying in business, because that's not going to work. I've come to the conclusion that this is just a fact of life.

Finally, if a woman or a guy gets targeted as a crier, he or she could be doomed. It's just bad for business.

Chapter 97

"GET OVER YOURSELF, STEVE"

I recently wrote a column regarding women crying in business. The day after it ran, I received at least a dozen e-mails from women criticizing me.

One that really got my attention came from Deb Di Gregorio, president and CEO of Camarés Communications. Said Di Gregorio, "Get over yourself, Steve! No crying in business? Says who? You, a man? . . . If we had listened to your tawdry argument 20 years ago, there would have been no place for women in business, no place for a balanced work/personal life . . . no time for men to leave work to see their kids play little league. . . . Women in the workforce have ignited dynamic and extraordinarily positive shifts in how business is conducted. Tears? Get over it buddy. You might well benefit from the freedom of being 'weak'—or you might discover, as women have known for eons, that the ability to cry publicly and freely is the source of our strength."

Deb's e-mail had me rethinking the crying in business issue. I talked to several women who offered feedback similar to Deb's. In retrospect, I think I came on a bit too strong in the original column. My intention was to make the point that being overly emotional in the workplace causes real problems, not just for the person who cries, but for the person raising the issue that causes the crying.

It's funny that not a single guy responded to that column. Guys don't think much about this stuff. Most men show their emotion or anger in ways other than crying. Of course, this is a generalization, but guys tend to show their emotion by raising their voice or occasionally using profanity. A few guys said to me that they thought I was nuts for saying that women shouldn't cry in the workplace because it wasn't politically correct. Okay, but my intent was not to offend women in the workplace, but rather to raise a legitimate issue that doesn't get talked about very often. I realize now that there was a much better, more thoughtful way to do it. My goal was to get men and women to think about this issue and find some productive ways to deal with it.

But the problem remains: certain leaders—like me—have a tendency to come on pretty strong on occasion. We do raise our voices. We do use "assertive" language like, "This is bullshit." Is that okay? Probably not. But I have come to realize that the best way to deal with things that go wrong in the workplace (or at home) is not to react right away. Take a breath and ask yourself: "What exactly am I angry about and what needs to happen in order to resolve the situation?" When you do that, you tend to be less reactionary. Less strident. Another benefit is that you move away from a blaming mentality, which is so destructive.

When you play the "blame game" everyone loses. That's the key. It's like you have to turn a switch on in your brain and go from asking the question, "Who screwed up?" to "Hey, what do we need to do about this?" If you don't turn that switch, you tend to overreact and cause unnecessary turmoil on your workplace team.

So what about the women, and men, who are overly sensitive to criticism in the workplace and who take it very personally? Some will say,

"But it IS personal, it is directed at ME." Yes and no. While it may be directed at you, most criticism is about a workplace situation or problem that has to be resolved. That's not personal. The more you personalize and internalize it, the more likely you are to get overly emotional, which gets in the way of moving forward and resolving the situation.

The sooner you acknowledge that you may have mishandled a situation or screwed up, the more likely it is to disarm the person challenging you. We are only human. We all make mistakes. I know I do.

Since my original "crying" column I've taken a much closer look at how aggressive I can be in certain situations, thereby evoking an overly emotional response in others. I was being too easy on myself and others who occasionally (if not more often) raise our voices to show our displeasure with a situation and direct it toward a particular employee. It's ironic that in the original column I said there was no place for being overly emotional in the workplace. In retrospect, that is exactly what I have been guilty of at times. Raising my voice. Scolding. Blaming. Sometimes even ridiculing. Frankly, being unnecessarily emotional. Crying isn't the only way to show emotion.

The bottom line is that all of us, regardless of gender, need to take a closer look at how our emotions impact those around us. The other lesson I've learned is to take a bigger step back before filing any column to make sure that the way I've said something is the best way to say it. What can I say? You live and learn.

Mailbag

Chapter 98

KNOWLEDGE IS IMPORTANT
BUT PASSION IS THE KEY

Check out this letter from Tom Vishia, who had some strong criticism of a column examining the importance of passion when communicating in public. Tom says, "I'm a communications consultant with over 30 years experience. . . . We do a lot of work on presentation skills and I respectfully disagree with your premise, Steve, that communicating 'clearly' has more to do with your passion about the topic than anything else. . . . It's all about skills and coaching. . . . Caring about something without the requisite skills will still result in an ineffective and unclear message."

Tom, you have to learn to get out of your shell and say what you really think! Your comments are appreciated, except I never said having skills and tools weren't important to improving your public speaking. I wrote that having all the communication skills in the world without passion makes for a pretty uninspiring presentation. Passion remains the missing ingredient for all too many well-intentioned professionals when communicating in the workplace.

Joe Sutton works for a communications company in New York and has some real concerns about the internal communication at his firm. "Some problems we encounter are no returns on e-mails, meetings moved up without consulting the involved parties, and conference calls that drag on and on." He also says that one of the biggest problems is that upper management distances itself from the majority of the company. He asks, "How does someone communicate that their boss's communication is terrible when they apparently don't want to hear it? Or do they?"

That's a tough one, Joe. I suggest you organize an informal brown-bag lunch with your coworkers and some key decision makers in the company. The purpose of the session should be to have an open, candid, and productive discussion about specific ways to address the above-mentioned communication issues in the company. Check out our web site, www.stand-deliver.com, for a past column on facilitating dialogue.

An article on constructive feedback prompted Rich Biddulph to respond this way. "Here's a cardinal rule I've incorporated over my career and it presumes that most all employees are trying their best but are not perfect: Always remind an employee of what they do well and always provide the criticism of shortcomings in a positive manner. . . . There has to be some positive attribute of all employees and they need to be reminded of that." Rich uses the following phrase that he says has been helpful, "I appreciate how you _____ during this project. You can be more effective in the next project if you _____."

Rich, your approach of looking for the positive in people is refreshing. Let's hope that others will take your advice and follow suit.

Rhoda Joseph, a former educator, wrote about the importance of schools helping young people reach their potential as confident and compelling communicators. "Schools could do much to give students a sense of ease in all forms of oral expression whether they involve interviews, speeches or one-to-one conversations. As a poet and writer, I derive considerable satisfaction in sharing poems and views in group settings. I credit imaginative and caring teachers for providing me with the motivation to do so."

Rhoda, you are so right. So many of the communication habits that we take into the workplace are a product of what we were taught in school. I see it beginning with my twelve-year-old son. Unfortunately, many of those habits have not been particularly helpful. Clearly in your case, that didn't happen.

Chapter 99

READING FROM THE SCRIPT

I got lots of great feedback to the column on the danger of scripting your presentations and reading verbatim.

Educational administrator Anthony Molinaro agrees that speeches are better when they are not read verbatim. "People need to believe in you as a person before they will believe in what you are trying to convey. . . . It seems so basic, but too many supposedly 'effective' speakers continue to read rather than speak from the heart. As a person who speaks to our youth on a regular basis, it is paramount that my audience believes in me more than the facts and figures I am speaking about."

You've got it right, Anthony. Students get inundated with information, rules, and standard-operating procedures. The educators who have the greatest impact are the ones that don't hide their passion. That's hard to do when they are glued to that script, regardless of what the content matter is.

Pat Bartling, a research librarian, has a great technique for preparing for any presentation. Says Pat, "I first write a very detailed beginning that grabs the audience and then add as much detail as I feel I need for the remainder of my talk. I then convert my notes to a bulleted outline, and rehearse my talk from that. This allows me to alter the talk as I go along, according to the reaction of the audience. What good is a live presentation if you cannot connect with the audience?"

Pat's comments prove that great presentations aren't about shooting from the hip or winging it, as some people think. In fact, it takes a lot more preparation and hard work to deliver a great five-minute presentation than it does to ramble on for fifty minutes. Getting to the great five minutes is about editing, prioritizing, and making some tough choices.

Nick Giuditta, an attorney, also says the outline approach works for him. "I write out my outline and then practice the speech numerous times without notes or reading from a script. Actually, the first person that taught me this was my fifth-grade teacher. Yet, it still amazes me to see educated people speak from a written document while never or rarely making eye contact. This is extremely ineffective and beyond amateurish in the business, professional or political world. Hopefully, more people will take your advice."

Think about how much impact Nick's fifth-grade teacher had on his professional teaching style. It's amazing what one teacher who really understands the art of communication can do. Conversely, consider how many kids get terrible advice from their teachers. (For example, "Focus on a spot six inches above the heads of your audience instead of making direct eye contact." Don't laugh; one of my son's grade-school teachers told him just that.)

One correspondent, who conducts seminars and workshops, has found that treating a prepared script as if you were an actor is most beneficial. Says Barry, "The primary reason this works is because you then have an objective. It is important for a speaker to figure out 'why' I want to accomplish a specific objective and then move on to 'how' he or she is going to accomplish this objective. . . . Audiences receive information when their emotions are open. If the audience is responding, they are with you. Good actors always do that."

You got it, reader. Have you ever noticed how actors will ask their director, "What's my motivation?" The key is to get in touch with what reaction you are trying to get from your audience. Once you do that, your presentation is likely to be a lot more effective.

Chapter 100

CUE CARDS, MOTIVATION, AND PRESIDENTIAL BLUNDERS

Dee Fazio wrote in with some tips on giving a small-group presentation. Fazio says she puts "cue cards" strategically around the room, which identify key topics. "For example, when speaking about a certain software, I have at least five things that I wanted to mention in bullets up on the wall. This also helps the audience to remember what you are speaking about because they visually see the topics." Fazio says that she also uses the audience to add new information to the material so that she can use it in future presentations. She says that by doing this, it allows you to stay away from written scripts and to play to your audience.

What a great idea, Dee. In my seminars I like to write information on flip chart pages and post them up as we go. However, I am going to try your cue card approach in the near future.

Lisa Smith wrote in response to a column on motivating employees. Says Smith, "The timing of your column was perfect relative to today's culture in most companies that have undergone downsizing and expense reduction and are now trying to re-energize the team." In her current position, Smith was asked to participate in an initiative to energize, motivate, engage, and encourage the group to become a winning team. "We kicked off surveys and focus groups to get a pulse of the group, and the majority of the responses focused around accountability and empowerment. Do you have any ideas for building action plans in these two areas?"

Yes. First, ask participants to come up with their own personal definition of "accountability" and "empowerment." Then ask each of them to develop a concrete example or scenario that supports their description. Your goal is to make these concepts more tangible, which will then allow you and your colleagues to develop practical action plans. These action plans can then be used to produce solid results.

Harriet Diamond recently retired as president of Diamond Associates, a consulting company she founded in 1985, and wrote in regarding a column on one of President Bush's press conferences. Says Diamond, "As I watched President Bush mismanage that conference I was incredulous not only at his lack of humility and acceptance of responsibility but also at how poorly he had been prepared. I am truly saddened by yet another blatant example of how our top executive is such a fertile model for poor communication, nonexistent team work and ineffective leadership."

Harriet, I wouldn't go as far as you go regarding teamwork and leadership; however, I still maintain that the president, or any executive with a lot of responsibility, should be more willing to acknowledge mistakes publicly and communicate directly as to what he has learned and his plans for the future. On that count, President Bush missed a huge opportunity when asked about his biggest mistake.

Chapter 101

COMMUNICATING WITH THE MEDIA TAKES DISCIPLINE

A reader recently wrote: "You argued recently that [the NFL's New York] Giant's rookie Jeremy Shockey should do a better job communicating with the media. You also said if you are honest with the media, they will give you a fair shot. But the media frequently takes things out of context; it's one of their favorite ploys. Isn't taking things out of context a form of deliberate lying? How should people who have to communicate with the media avoid having their words twisted?"

Yes, I agree that the media—newspapers included—sometimes "take things out of context." But that's not the issue. Most people who have problems communicating effectively through this medium are not disciplined enough. One of the biggest reasons people get upset when they see themselves quoted in print or as part of a television or radio news story is because they rambled on and on without a clear, concise, focused message. Consider this example:

A few years ago, the former dean of an international affairs and diplomacy school at a major university gave an interview to a *Star Ledger* reporter. It was supposed to be a feature story promoting the new school. The reporter happened to ask about international customs and traditions having to do with food and attire. The dean went on for about ten minutes talking about which countries expect you to take your shoes off before a meal and which countries set a table a certain way. When the story came out, it sounded like the university was running an international charm school. The dean was livid. He wanted the *Ledger* to print a retraction. The fact is he had no beef with the reporter or the newspaper. He was the one who said all those things and went on in detail about international customs. Yet, he was there to talk about the mission and the message of a new school that would be training future diplomats in international relations. That's the message he was supposed to get across. That's the message he should have stayed on. But because the dean, like so many others who are forced to deal with the media, was undisciplined and unfocused, he, the new school, and the university paid the price. Your goal is not to ignore an off-the-mark or seemingly irrelevant question, but rather to answer very briefly and then move back to the main message you want to get across. That's disciplined communication.

TIP TO REMEMBER—When communicating with the media or dealing with a Q & A forum, be it a meeting, seminar, or when making a presentation, your main message is your *anchor*. It should ground all of your communication. Your audience can't handle, nor can they remember, a half-dozen different points you want to get across. You also lose control when you talk about so many different topics. You leave it to the audience members (or media representatives) to pick which point they choose to focus on. If their impression or opinion as to what is important or interesting isn't the one you wanted them to focus on, whose fault is that? When this happens, you as the communicator will say you were "taken out of context." But were you really? Didn't you say what you are quoted as saying? That's not being taken out of context. How is the audience supposed to read your mind?

When communicating in this type of situation have your main message at the tip of your tongue. Remember why you are there and what you want people to walk away remembering. If you keep that in mind and communicate accordingly, you will be amazed at the results.

Chapter 102

MANAGEMENT TIPS FOR THE YOUNGER BOSS

One reader raises an issue that is increasingly common for older professionals in the workplace. Says this person, "Due to the current economy and 9/11, I was unemployed for 1½ years. I ended up taking a job in my chosen field, but for the first time in 20 years, I am now a line staff employee (not the Program Director) and making half the money I've previously made. My boss is half my age, only has a BA degree (I've got an MA) and has only been an administrator for 2 years. I am often tempted to advise my boss based on her lack of experience. What advice can you give to someone who is directly supervised by a boss who has far less experience in a specific field?"

This correspondent is not alone. More and more older professionals have lost their managerial jobs and have reentered the workplace in positions with less authority. Your best bet is to take a positive attitude regarding the situation and offer to be helpful to your younger boss. Tell her that you respect her opinion on a specific issue, but also share your experience when dealing with a similar situation in your career. Tell her you want her to benefit from the mistakes you've made through the years. Don't patronize or talk down to her. Just let her know that you know how hard her job really is and that you want her to succeed.

Melissa Brenner (a pseudonym since this reader asked to remain anonymous) wrote that a recent column on micromanaging touched her. Says Melissa, "I am a conscientious employee and very detail oriented. Recently, due to these skills I've been asked to extend my 'management' to all current projects within the company, which has become time consuming." Says a frustrated Melissa, "I don't feel productive when I spend so much time checking up on other people. Our close-knit group of long-time employees is beginning to unravel. I'm uncomfortable in my new role and I know my co-workers are feeling the same. Any tips, Steve?"

Obviously, Melissa, you are a classic victim of your own success. Why not tell your boss that given your new role and added responsibilities, you are concerned about the impact this will have on your ability to perform at the level of excellence you expect of yourself. Let him know you appreciate his confidence in your abilities, but that you would love to see other team members grow and develop their skills as well. Offer to work directly with them as a coach/mentor in the areas you are particularly strong in. Help him to see what he cannot see for himself. Hopefully he will get it, but even if he doesn't, you can only learn from the experience.

One executive responded to a recent column on the need for leaders to lead, not be liked. "An important skill for any leader is specific feedback. When a leader makes a statement to an individual or group, he must convey why the statement is being made, why it is important and a brief history leading up to that moment. . . . Specific feedback usually follows a SMART pattern (Specific, Measurable, Attainable, Relevant, and Timely)." This reader went on to say that he disagreed with that column's recommendation to "keep socializing to specific situations." Instead, he believes that social interaction is "dependent upon the job, work environment and the leader's personality. One of the key elements missing in today's work place is a sense of community."

You raised several good points, Dave, and I can't disagree with any of them. Thanks for the SMART feedback.

Chapter 103

READERS RESPOND TO PARCELLS, TORRE, AND BOSS STEINBRENNER

One column profiled the "confrontational" leadership style of former New York Jets and Giants coach Bill Parcells. Some of Parcells's more memorable quotes in a *Harvard Business Review* article include "Don't wait to earn your leadership; impose it . . . apply pressure—that's the only thing that any of us really responds to." And "I relish confrontation, not because it makes me feel powerful, but because it provides an opportunity to get things straight with people." The question is, How does Parcells's leadership style translate off the football field? Here are some readers' reactions:

One person writes, "The corporate person is generally one who respects fellow workers and speaks in a kind and acceptable manner; it is a person who desires to ingratiate him- or herself so as to keep their job secure and advance in position as far as talents permit. Thus, the management approach is more genteel, although forceful, in its attempt to make the worker understand what the goals are to be achieved. [In a noncorporate world], Bill Parcells has the way and methods that are successful in getting through to his players and thus he achieves success on the field of play. He talks 'their language.' He taunts them, he berates them, and he shouts at them and otherwise treats them in a similar way to the way they themselves treat their fellow players on the field and particularly those players on the opposing teams."

This correspondent has an interesting point about each profession having its own set of rules and unique culture. Yet, one wonders whether there are certain universal do's and don't's, wrongs or rights of leadership and communication that provide lessons for all of us. What do you think?

Another reader adds this: "Parcells's confrontational style was only effective because he also set a vision for his players both in terms of what the goal was and also of what he expected from each of them. I doubt that there was any question in anyone's mind that he expected 100 percent effort and execution. They also respected his knowledge of the game and ability to get the most out of his players. Although I don't agree with his style and recognize that it wouldn't work for me, I believe that he was a very effective leader."

This person is absolutely right. Like most leaders, Parcells is a complex guy, yet clearly, his "in your face" approach is what he is most recognized for.

Another reader responded to the Parcells article but also commented on a recent piece praising the communication skills of Yankees' manager Joe Torre and criticizing those of Yankees' owner George Steinbrenner. He wrote, "I think the management style depends upon the situation or game. The best leadership style is to give tips to a player and see how he handles the tips. If he fails, it is shown in the boxscore."

This person has an interesting perspective that clearly has value beyond the world of sports. However, while I agree with them about situational leadership, I'm not convinced that, long term, any professional in any arena will respond in a positive way to confrontation and intimidation.

Finally, another reader got right to the point when he wrote, "Bill Parcells is your classic loud-mouth, à la former Indiana University basketball coach Bobby Knight and the late Billy Martin. Joe Torre is the perfect example of getting the job done and still remaining an intelligent and classy human being. I think you should write a book on communications and send the first copy to Bill Parcells."

The Billy Martin reference isn't totally clear to me. As for Bob Knight, I don't care how many games he won at Indiana—no coach, no leader has the right to physically, mentally, and emotionally abuse his team players, particularly college athletes who aren't being paid to perform.

Chapter 104

PLAYING AT WORK

A reader writes: "I just got finished reading your article on attitude. I work for a company that is based out of New York and we have just incorporated into our daily routine the "Fish" philosophy (from the Pike Fish Market in Seattle) of "Play." What suggestions do you have for playing in the workplace?"

FISH! is a great book and video that I have featured in my writings. Playing in the workplace is extremely important in creating an environment in which people are working together and giving their all. Sometimes people hear the concept of "play" and think it means not being serious about your product or service, much less your customers. This couldn't be further from the truth.

Consider creating a work environment that is loose and relaxed, but deadly serious about quality performance and service. Try celebrating the birthdays of team members with a cake and a break from the daily routine. Or, try taking staff members out for lunch—it can pay big dividends. Either of these playful activities sends the message that your people are worth the time and money. It also allows them to break bread and enjoy each other in a social setting. Beyond doing lunch, your team might also consider getting together outside the workplace where no business is discussed. You can start a softball team or join a bowling league. It doesn't matter what the activity is, as long as you are having fun and in the process getting to know each other just a little bit better. If done with a positive attitude (as opposed to mandating it), such playful activities have the potential of producing a dynamite team that not only plays well together, but works together toward a common goal.

Another reader writes: "I'm a recent college graduate and I work at an entry-level job where my primary responsibility is to oversee a staff of ten. They vary in age and educational background. I am young, inexperienced and eager to learn. What can I do to help build a quality team?"

Beyond the playing that we just discussed, consider how you are going to handle meetings with your team. First, don't hold meetings unless you absolutely have to. One of the worst things you can do as a young (or older) manager is to hold meetings just for the sake of it. Your people will resent you for it and those meetings will wind up being counterproductive.

Next, when you do hold a meeting, make sure the meeting never lasts for more than an hour. The key is to not have too many items on the agenda and keep the conversation focused on the issue at hand. As the meeting facilitator, make sure your meetings are interactive and engaging and you as the manager don't do all or even most of the talking. Send the message that you genuinely care about the feedback and input of your team.

Another thing you can do is put individual team members together on specific projects. This will encourage them to work together and get to know each other. Coach their efforts and make yourself accessible without being a pest and looking over their shoulders. Then, when the individual mini-teams successfully complete a project, make sure you acknowledge those efforts to the larger team. The key is to create a positive feeling as early as possible and minimize the all-too-typical back-biting, finger-pointing, and petty politics that plague so many teams. Your attitude and behavior will be the biggest factors in how your team performs. The fact that you are starting so young as a manager and taking this responsibility so seriously is a very positive sign.

Chapter 105

PEOPLE SKILLS AND LISTENING TIPS

Following is some feedback from my column on people skills as well as some advice on a listening pet peeve.

Ron Reich, a leadership development trainer, wrote in response to a column on people skills, saying, "I agree with you that relationships are key to success. However, I disagree with your advice regarding the 'golden rule.' As you stated, the golden rule teaches, 'treat others as you would want them to treat you.'"

According to Ron, the "platinum rule" is much more effective and useful. He says the platinum rule calls for treating others as they want to be treated. Reich recommends that a manager determine how his or her peers prefer to be treated and then use that style with them.

Ron, you raise a lot of interesting points, but as for the so-called platinum rule, in reality there are often too many people in an organization to treat them exactly how you think they would want to be treated. In my column, I assumed that the vast majority of professionals would want to be treated fairly and, therefore, it is a safe assumption to assume others want the same thing. Maybe it's a case of coming down to a combination of the golden rule and the platinum rule, which would make it, I guess, the silver rule.

Another suggestion on how to improve your people skills under stress came from a reader who has over four decades in network TV and radio. He zeroed in on people who too often become abrasive when deadline pressures are approaching. He says, "In the news arena, these pressures mount each day. As a result, years ago I coined an expression for people working with me in those pressure-cooker situations—Poise Under Pressure (PUP)."

This person swears by the PUP theory, which emphasizes maintaining composure when things get a little tough or stressful on the job. He insists on taking a moment to regroup before blowing off some steam, whether you are "dealing with breaking news stories or up against a financial report deadline."

I really like the PUP theory. Sometimes we blow off steam thinking it's good for our mental health to get our frustration off our chest. I'm not so sure. This can sometimes turn off those around us. Instead, just taking that moment or two to regroup could pay big dividends in the workplace.

Barbara Rogers (a pseudonym since the actual reader asked not to be identified), who calls herself an avid listener, writes that there are still many challenges she faces when it comes to honing this important communication skill. "I am frequently interrupted by family members (and an occasional neighbor) when I am speaking to them. I've explained to them that it is rude to interrupt, only to hear responses such as,

'Interrupting is part of conversation' or 'You are rude for telling me not to interrupt.' Do you have any suggestions for coping with my pet peeve? Is it because I am dealing with family members that this is becoming such a challenge? Help!"

Dear avid listener—trust me, it is not just your family. Incessant interrupting is one of the most common communication faux pas. The reasons people do it are endless, but it largely centers around being overly self-centered, terribly impatient, and downright rude. My suggestion is that you calmly but clearly tell those who constantly interrupt you exactly how you feel when they do it. Then, draw a line in the sand and let them know that you'd rather not converse with them until they decide they are going to try to interrupt less.

Chapter 106

THE BOTTOM LINE ON LISTENING

Following is a sampling of what some readers had to say in response to a listening quiz given by the *Star-Ledger*'s Business section.

Marilyn Rohrbach says, "Several years ago, 'active listening' was a huge tool—'probing' questions, confirming statements and body language that confirmed understanding were the recommendations. I never was a fan of that technique because it seemed somewhat phony and rehearsed. I do, however, find myself giving the impression of being in a hurry. Whether this is actually true or not, I am a 'get-to-the-point' kind of person in my professional life and much more relaxed in my personal life."

Marilyn adds, "Professionally, I also find myself asking some probing questions to confirm my interest and understanding, which is part of the old 'active listening,' but many times don't really listen to the answer."

The key, Marilyn, is not to simply appear to be listening, but to actually listen. Faking it won't get it done. What people need to realize is that deciding to listen is an investment that can pay huge dividends. Through exceptional listening, we find out about the needs, wants, fears, and hopes of others. Finding these things out allows you to provide quality customer service and enhance your relationships. That's what makes it worth it.

Sheila Beers says, "The 'sentence-finisher' is so annoying. That person is either immature or completely arrogant. Either way, it leads to a frustrating situation. Also, I find that focusing attention on a response rather than the nature of the conversation is usually a by-product of nervousness or trying to impress. Confidence and learning to relax are in order. Of course, in an 'interview' scenario, this is easier said than done."

Sheila says accepting constructive criticism is hard for her. "If you can learn to accept constructive criticism, it will be your best friend. Learn from it, use it and capitalize on it. Good listening is a product of a conscious decision. I liken that to maintaining a good marriage—you have to make a conscious effort to work at it every day (especially after 25 years)!"

Hey Sheila, you make a great point about the connection between good listening and maintaining a good marriage. In that spirit, consider what Debbie Granrath had to say on the subject of constructive criticism. "I become defensive and shut out the rest of what is being said as opposed to seeing feedback as an opportunity to grow. I also become angry with the person. . . ."

You're not alone, Debbie. A lot of us become defensive when we are criticized. Obviously praise is a lot easier to hear. Do you notice we never interrupt when someone is telling us how great we are? It's all in your frame of mind. As opposed to saying to yourself, "How dare you criticize me?" consider a different approach: "Thanks, I needed that." (Even if it doesn't feel good to hear it.)

Becoming defensive is a product of our insecurities, which often come from our childhood, but if we can get past some of that, the floodgates can be opened to valuable insights and observations from others as to how we might improve in a given area. And all of us, regardless of how great we think we are, can do better.

Finally, once you get in the habit of thanking people who give you "constructive" criticism or feedback, it can become second nature. The bottom line, be it listening, speaking, or any communication technique, is to develop good habits and minimize those that aren't so great—one day at a time.

Chapter 107

CHILDREN OFFER INSIGHT ON MANAGING ANGER

Past "mailbag columns" have featured letters from professionals in business, education, and the nonprofit arena. But awhile back, I got some feedback I frankly didn't expect. A teacher from a grammar school in Union County, New Jersey, wrote that he was struck by my column on managing anger and apparently made it required reading for all of his students. Not only did I offer advice on dealing with anger, but I also confessed to communicating in a less than professional way when my anger got the best of me. Some of this teacher's students decided to respond to that column.

Out of the mouth of babes. Remember, all of these kids are fifth-graders.

"Dealing with anger is something we should all learn how to do because everyone gets angry about something. Your article had some good ideas, but I think the best way is patience."

Great advice. Patience is something we all could use a little more of in this fast-paced world. Through staying on top of our emotions and thinking before we (over)react, we can avoid taking our anger out on others.

In one of my writings on anger management, I recounted an incident in which I raised my voice with one of my staff about something that had gone wrong in front of several people in our office. One student wasn't impressed:

"Mr. Adubato, please don't yell at your staff. Too many people yell and scream and your staff probably works very hard. You don't have to yell at people just because they make one little mistake."

Ouch! Tell me what you really think. You are wise beyond your years.

"My mother has told me that the best way to solve a problem is to listen. I should listen to what each person has to say and then try to agree on the best answer to the problem. When a mistake is made, pointing fingers and pointing blame does not solve anything."

George Steinbrenner should take this child's advice. The key is, when mistakes occur, it is not always the result of a single person's actions. More commonly, it is a combination of things and/or some sort of miscommunication. When things go wrong, as this student recommends, a healthier approach is to work together as a team and find the best solution without creating a lot of bloodshed.

"I try my best not to get angry and also try to think first before I speak. But when I do get angry, sometimes I yell and scream and say things I don't mean. I sometimes blame others only later to find out that it was my own fault. I've learned that the best thing to do when I'm angry is to just walk away."

If this student keeps writing like that, the *Ledger* should give her her own column in the Business Edge section. One technique that I have learned when I begin feeling angry is to stop, count to ten (who am I kidding? I only count to three), and think to myself, "Will I really accomplish anything by expressing my anger right now?" The answer is usually the same. No. However, if you feel the uncontrollable urge to blow off some steam, take the advice and simply walk away. Trust me, once you cool down you'll be glad you did.

"Mr. Adubato, you shouldn't let little things get in your way and don't take things out on other people for things that you do."

I bet this student has been reading one of my favorite books by Richard Carlson, *Don't Sweat the Small Stuff and It's All Small Stuff*. The little things often snowball into big things, and then we can't remember why we even got angry in the first place.

I don't know about you, but I think that the students in this fifth-grade class are pretty smart.

Chapter 108

TOO LITTLE DATA TO JUDGE THE LEADERSHIP OF WOMEN

An executive who wrote in to me is also a diversity trainer and manager and responded to a recent column examining gender differences and their connection to communication styles in the workplace. "Gender is a complex issue. . . . The fact is more men are still heading up corporations globally, so how can we judge women in leadership fairly? If more women had a role of leadership then the key factors of personality, environment and choice could surface as data points for research. Until then, many of the diversity issues are still evident and the behaviors as a result of these issues still impact productivity and the 'bottom line.'"

You raise a great point, David. The sample size of women in executive positions is too small to make confident assessments of women's leadership and communication styles. Let's hope that changes very soon.

Michelle Vogel (a pseudonym), a financial manager for a small real estate company in California, has a serious concern regarding one of her assistants. Vogel says that there are many times her assistant will forget things or make mistakes on a project, even after she has explained step-by-step what needed to be done. Says Vogel, "I've tried talking to her about mistakes . . . but every method I've tried either falls on deaf ears or causes her to get defensive. . . . It has reached a point where I do a good portion of her duties myself, and the things still left to her, I have to quality control. Does this make me a micromanager or does this mean she's not a good assistant?"

The simple answer is both. However, I wouldn't beat myself up for staying on top of the situation. It just shows that you care a great deal. My advice is to establish a time frame. For example, for the next six months commit to being the best mentor you can be, providing concrete advice and feedback to your assistant. If she isn't where she needs to be by then, let her go and don't look back. (If it gets to that, remember, you don't have to be Donald "you're fired" Trump to get the job done.)

Mike Bianchi had a lot to say about multitasking and its impact on communication. "I find multitasking to be most objectionable when people are taking a phone call while having a conversation with me. Whether picking up the phone while speaking with me face-to-face or clicking over to call waiting, I instantly get the message that the current conversation with me is not important to them." Bianchi says that even though people feel they are being more efficient when they are handling interruptions, oftentimes tasks take longer overall and with poorer results.

If more people realized the price they pay for these actions, maybe they would think twice before doing it. Why not be proactive, Mike, and share your thoughts with selected professional colleagues? It could make a difference.

Captain Rich Naruszewicz wrote a very touching letter in response to a column on New Jersey Lottery director Ginny Bauer, who lost her husband David on September 11. "I am a captain on a high-speed ferry and Ginny's husband Dave got on my ferry every morning to go to Manhattan. Dave Bauer, 'Big Dave,' 'Gentle Dave' always smiled. I shook hands with him every morning . . . but I never saw Dave after that tragic day. . . . My hat goes off to Ginny Bauer and the rest of the people who lost a loved one on that day and carry on. She is a role model in my book."

Obviously, September 11 was a horrific tragedy, but leaders like Ginny Bauer have chosen to turn it into something positive, as hard as that is. Your letter proves that, Rich.

ABOUT THE AUTHOR

Steve Adubato, Ph.D., a four-time Emmy Award–winning television anchor on Thirteen/WNET New York (PBS), has a distinguished career as a newspaper columnist, broadcaster, author, motivational speaker, university lecturer, and communication coach. He lives in Montclair, New Jersey.